CUMBRIA LIBRARIES

D1331635

County Council

Libraries, books and more . . .

MORTON 5/17		
LOL		

Please return/renew this item by the last due date.
Library items may be renewed by phone on
030 33 33 1234 (24 hours) or via our website
www.cumbria.gov.uk/libraries

Cumbria Libraries

CLIC

Interactive Catalogue

Ask for a CLIC password

First published by

Independent Thinking Press
Crown Buildings, Bancyfelin, Carmarthen, Wales, SA33 5ND, UK
www.independentthinkingpress.com

Independent Thinking Press is an imprint of Crown House Publishing Ltd.

© Nick Tiley-Nunn 2014

The right of Nick Tiley-Nunn to be identified as the author of this work has been asserted
by him in accordance with the Copyright, Designs and Patents Act 1988.

First published 2014.

Illustrations © Les Evans, 2014

Les Evans has asserted his right under the Copyright, Designs and Patents Act 1988,
to be identified as illustrator of this work

Images page 154 © Snowshill - Fotolia.com, page 168 © fhphotographie - Fotolia.com, page 202 ©
pcelicamaja - Fotolia.com, page 213 © imagedb - Fotolia.com.

British Library Cataloguing-in-Publication Data
A catalogue entry for this book is available
from the British Library.

Print ISBN 978-1-78135-135-2
Mobi ISBN 978-1-78135-208-3
ePub ISBN 978-1-78135-209-0

Edited by Phil Beadle

Printed and bound in the UK by
Gomer Press, Llandysul, Ceredigion

ACKNOWLEDGEMENTS

My thanks go, first, to Dr Brendan Stones for being more inspiring than he will ever know. I would also like to thank Phil Beadle and all the wonderful staff at Crown House Publishing and Independent Thinking Ltd for taking a chance on me. Finally, I would like to thank my darling wife, Rachel, and all my family for helping me to keep putting one foot in front of the other. Without all of them this would never have happened.

CONTENTS

FOREWORD BY PHIL BEADLE

Nick Tiley-Nunn might be the best teacher in the world. He is certainly the best I've seen. Ever. I've never seen anyone, ever, who has gifts anywhere near the level he's quite so blithe and modest about. "I do my best," he shrugs with a disarming and ingenuous smile. Seated at the back of his class in a small room in an area of London I'm never really comfortable in, having taken a job doing a teaching and learning audit for a quite brilliant school, Radnor House, I witnessed, for probably the second time in my career, an untutorable genius at work. Halfway through the lesson, I turned round to an awestruck 9-year-old girl, who was learning about division through seeing how many sweets a shark might eat given the opportunity. I asked her a question, "Is he the best teacher in the world?" She was utterly certain, "Yehhhhhhhhh! Of course. Everyone knows that!"

My observation notes from the time noted: "This is the best maths lesson I have ever sat in on. The students adore him and rightly think he is the most brilliant teacher they have ever had. He has invented techniques that every maths teacher in the country could learn from, combines rote and kinaesthetic learning, which is something that only the most profoundly brilliant teachers are able to conceive of, and, like the masterful football player who vibrates on a different string to anyone else, has enough time on the ball to divert into accidentally teaching kids about alliteration. He is a stunning talent."

And this is not my opinion alone. Here is the view of one of Nick's former colleagues, Kate Ryan who currently leads a group of eminent educators in driving improvement in education systems globally: "Nick is simply unparalleled. He is limitless."

The idea of the 'How to Teach' series of books is that teachers encounter the geniuses of the form (next year there will be a book in this series by Darren Mead, perhaps the most significant thinker about teaching in Britain). Primary maths is not a realm I have any real knowledge of, but I know class when I see it, and Nick Tiley-Nunn, as a practitioner, is next level brilliant.

Of the man who wrote this book: he is unassuming, doesn't recognise the fact that he is even talented, and is the kind of quiet, deeply gentle and sweet man you would want your grown-up daughter to bring home. Where his genius came from, I don't know. It appears either a genetic accident or the result of a boisterous child who was taught, at school, that maths was really boring, and who wanted to prove it didn't have to be, and that it was a matter of the teacher's intent: their seriousness in finding the (surface level) frivolity. Wherever it came from, it is there, and I leave you to commune with it, and see if you agree with me; furthermore, to see if you can infect your class with the same total absence of boredom any child who is lucky enough to be taught by Mr Tiley-Nunn experiences every day.

INTRODUCTION

NUMERATE OR MATHEMATICALLY LITERATE?

I call one of my favourite lessons on teaching division,"Anyone can feed sweets to sharks" (I will explain later). It also serves as a metaphor for the way many of us feel when we first step into the classroom as teachers. When I started teaching, I was barely old enough to make my own packed lunch, and I remember the terror of entering a classroom full of 'sharks' waiting for me to 'feed' them 'sweeties' of knowledge. "What if I run out of sweets? What if they get a taste for teacher flesh? This is a bad idea! RUN!"

Some claim that they thrive on fear, some leave the profession because of it, but all teachers have felt its icy finger at some point. It's a universal teaching experience. For primary teachers, it doesn't matter that the 'sharks' are only little – they still bite!

We've all got our own specialisms and deficiencies: there are elements of the job we feel confident about and elements where we feel a bit out of our depth. For the majority of primary teachers, one subject, above all others, fills us with trepidation and fear: mathematics – the Marmite subject.

I wasn't the most successful mathematician at school. I was alright when it was just about simple arithmetic: my brain could punch out answers at a fair rate. However, when it came to writing down my workings, the game was up. Everything about this more formal approach to mathematics seemed to be an elaborate plot devised to make me look like a muppet. Getting my unwieldy numerical scrawlings to fit into neat little boxes was a problem; I was struggling to keep my writing on the page, let alone in strict cm² cells and neatly aligned in columns. I persevered with it, though, because I wanted to be a good boy and to do well at school. However, lessons spent trying to work out how much Sanjay was going to pay for a bag of apples were wasted on me; I was too busy working out whether I was going to be a Power Ranger or one of the X-Men at breaktime.

The real shame is that I wasn't 'bad' at maths, I just never caught the bug: numbers written neatly in grid-lined exercise books couldn't compete for me with the fizzes and bangs of science, the gruesome accounts of battles won and lost in history, the exploration of stunning landscapes and cultures in geography, the endlessly entrancing stories of English or, most notably, the thrill of chasing a ball around a sports field. To be honest, even French lessons, with their seemingly never-ending learning of tenses, were above maths in my hierarchy of subjects that I cared about.

Throughout my school life, there were very few memorable maths moments. I remember making an awesome macaroni abacus in Year 1, and there was the time in Year 3 when Charlie almost choked on a Unifix cube and threw up over the desk. In Year 6, we had to measure the dimensions of the classroom and didn't have any tape measures, so we created the longest ruler known to man, which at morning break became the longest lightsabre known to man.

The secondary school years were worse. Confined to the realms of mediocrity in set four out of seven, I whiled away each lesson hoping that the teacher would not linger too long over my workings for fear that his body odour was contagious. Even so-called 'project work' was reduced to working out how much a school trip to the zoo would cost or measuring the height and shoe size of the pupils in my class. The highlight would be the occasional trip to computer room to create a spreadsheet to demonstrate our 'findings'. If I could sum up my maths education as a colour it would be beige, as a flavour it would be tapioca, and as a hobby it would be coin collecting. The most worrying thing was that I knew maths was supposed to be important, but I couldn't see how or why: it was neither culturally nor contextually rich. For me, maths just never added up. You could not have paid me to study mathematics after GCSEs, a sentiment which was shared by all of my class as none of us went on to study maths further.

WHY DON'T PEOPLE LIKE MATHS?

The majority of primary teachers have not studied mathematics at a higher level. In fact, I would probably go a step further and say that there are more primary teachers who actively dislike maths than enjoy it. There are a lot of primary teachers who would not teach maths if they had any choice at all. They didn't like it when they were at school as a pupil, and don't like it now they are a teacher. They didn't excel in it then, and don't excel in it now.

The social stigma attached to being 'bad at maths' is less pronounced than that of being illiterate. The charity, National Numeracy, carries out an annual survey into adults' attitudes towards maths and numeracy in the UK. The most recent survey, carried out in March 2014, highlights several important points for consideration.[1] First, where 66% of UK adults stated that they would feel embarrassed to tell someone that they were bad at literacy related tasks, only 48% of people would feel the same about telling someone that they were bad at maths. Perhaps of even greater concern is that among those who rated their maths skills as poor, 45% believed that maths is more innate than a learned skill.

---

1   See National Numeracy, YouGov Survey Findings (12 March 2014). Available at: http://www.nationalnumeracy.org.uk/resources/134/index.html.

Take a moment to consider the message this sends to the children in our classrooms. Over half of the adults in the UK would not be embarrassed to admit that they are poor at maths, and almost half the people who consider themselves to be poor at maths believe that it is mostly down to them not drawing a winning ticket in the genetic lottery. "Well, I was never any good at maths, so what chance has he got?" is a phrase we hear all too often at parents' evenings. Some are even prepared to completely write off their children's mathematical ability at the slightest hint of difficulty in the subject. Another alarming aspect is that this mindset seems to be something that is more prevalent in the UK than in other developed countries.

Chris Humphries, the chair of National Numeracy, is on record as saying, "It is simply inexcusable for anyone to say 'I can't do maths'. It's a peculiarly British disease."[2] And the National Centre for Excellence in the Teaching of Mathematics, in one of their activity packs,[3] makes reference to a discussion about mathematics between academics at an international conference, where an admission of, "Oh, I can't do maths to save my life!" by a British academic is met with sympathetic laughter by the other Brits, but with utter shock from non-English academics, one of whom responds, "We are very surprised to hear you make such an admission in public. It is very embarrassing." The discussion develops further with the explanation that admitting weakness in maths in British society is, "an acceptable thing to do and even makes you sound like a 'good egg'".

Despite this gloomy outlook on our view of maths in the UK, I believe that there is a relatively straightforward solution. Put simply, children who enjoy mathematics are more likely to perform well.

---

2   See National Numeracy, 17m Adults Have Poor Numeracy Skills (press release, 28 February 2012). Available at: http://www.nationalnumeracy.org.uk/news/9/index.html.

3   National Centre for Excellence in the Teaching of Mathematics, Attitudes to Mathematics Activity Pack B: Working with a School Whole Staff Event (n.d.). Available at: https://www.ncetm.org.uk/public/files/2990088/Attitudes%2bto%2bMathematics%2bActivity%2bPack%2bB.pdfB.pdf.

So, what are we going to do about it?

This book is intended to be your solution to the knotty issue of making maths enjoyable for your pupils, and the first step in this is your own attitude to maths! From here on in, I will model the positive mindset that you will need if you are going to make maths as exciting as it can be. Step one is to view yourself as outstanding, or as having the potential to be. By picking up this little collection of ramblings you have made the first step: you are clearly interested in what you do and want to be better at it. This was exactly how I felt about teaching maths. I realised I had a deficiency, and that only thinking positively about it would start me on the road to being any good at it.

Maths is the 'Cinderella' subject of the primary curriculum. It is not the ugly sister that it is often presented as being; it can be the 'Belle of the Ball' if the correct make-up is applied. This book will show you what 'make-up' you can slap on the subject to make it alluring for young people, and will hopefully encourage you to dress mathematics up in the way that best suits you and your pupils.

MATHS VERSUS NUMERACY

A core issue with primary maths is the lack of agreement over what is actually important. The terms numeracy and mathematics are used interchangeably, and many argue that they are one and the same. If we treat numeracy in the same way as literacy, then it's about having the necessary mathematical ability to get by in everyday life. Activities such as being able to add up the cost of the food in your shopping basket and read a train timetable are undoubtedly important, and primary education has an integral part to play in the development of these core skills.

However, I don't really like the term numeracy, or the attitudes that come about as a result of the education system's use of it. The foregrounding of numeracy has us fixated, as a profession, on the four operations of addition, subtraction, multiplication and division. Of course, simple arithmetic is important, but there is rather more to maths than these four operations. Imagine the state of the English curriculum if it concentrated solely on spelling or the geography curriculum dominated entirely by maps. Art is not just painting, music is not just learning the recorder, French is not just learning how to ask where the library is, history is not just the study of kings, religious education does not focus solely on Jesus and PE is not just about forgetting your kit. If the breadth of these subjects was similarly restricted, then how popular would they be with children? How popular would they be with teachers? This is why I feel a slight discomfort with the term numeracy: it highlights the emphasis on arithmetic; on the answer over the problem; on being either right or wrong; on the empirical over the creative.

Being numerate is important, but it shouldn't come at the cost of kids developing a genuine interest in the wider mathematical picture. Likewise, arithmetical skill should not come at the expense of highly developed problem-solving skills. Getting the right answer can be important, but we can learn an incredible amount through getting things wrong.

WHAT IS IMPORTANT IN PRIMARY MATHS?

In my opinion, we must strive to build the foundations of mathematical literacy as outlined by PISA:

> Mathematical literacy is an individual's capacity to identify and understand the role that mathematics plays in the world, to make well-founded judgements and to use and engage with mathematics in ways that meet the needs of that individual's life as a constructive, concerned and reflective citizen.[4]

We need to escape from the black and white nature of right and wrong answers and place significantly more importance on the process. I referred earlier to the idea of feeding sharks: what if the sharks were given the opportunity to feed themselves? If a key educational objective is to prepare the next generation of adults to take an active role within society, we have to ask what sort of citizens we want: human calculators or creative thinkers with a practised penchant for problem-solving?

So, back to you dear reader. Regardless of your mathematical ability, one thing I will bet my protractor on is that you're a fantastic problem-solver. It's what you do on a daily basis, it's sewn into the fabric of our profession. On any given day, we deal with an ever-increasing set of problems and attempt to solve them. Some of these problems are pretty straightforward ("David, your handwriting will definitely improve if you hold your pencil with your hand rather than your left nostril.") but others are more difficult, requiring us to take in the often multifaceted nature of the problem before deciding on an appropriate plan of attack. A teacher without problem-solving skills is

---

4   Organisation for Economic Co-operation and Development, *Assessing Scientific, Reading and Mathematical Literacy: A Framework for PISA 2006* (Paris: OECD, 2006), p. 72.

about as useful as a helicopter ejector seat. If all of us in the profession share this universal skill, it seems silly not to harness it to improve our teaching of primary maths.

WHY PROBLEM-SOLVING IS IMPORTANT AND HOW TO ENGAGE PUPILS IN IT

Child A: Errrrrrrm, sir, I think we've got a problem ...

Teacher: Really? Show me what the problem is.

Child B (head stuck inside a cardboard box): I'm stuck! I tried to see if it was the right size for my head, and it's a bit tight. I can't pull it off!

Teacher: Fantastic! Tell me what you're going to do next to solve the problem.

Problems. They are more prevalent than sand in the desert and salt in the sea. And, much like primary mathematics, they are labelled as negatives: we approach them with negativity and view them as a barrier. Given the opportunity to rub a magic lamp and be granted three wishes, many of us might wish for some form of problem to vanish. This is perfectly understandable because problems make life bumpy. Yet it is precisely this bumpiness that has yielded some of the most exceptional human beings and creations that have ever graced our planet. Without water pouring through the hull of the *Syracusia*, Archimedes would not have developed his engineering masterpiece, the Archimedean screw; without the need for an instant and practical light source, Thomas Edison would not have developed the first light bulb; without the problem of how to create multiple copies of books, Johannes Gutenberg would not have created the first printing press with moveable type.

Without problems, these solutions would have never come to fruition. Like a comic book hero and his nemesis, solutions are nothing without the problem that existed in the first place. We need to treat problems as a mechanism for improvement rather than something that gets in the way of success. By exposing our young learners to problems on a regular basis we not only increase enthusiasm and passion for the subject, but also lay the foundations for creating independent, resilient and skilful learners.

WHAT IS THE GOAL?

Why is problem-solving relegated to the substitutes' bench? It is a bit like that flamboyant play-maker who has the ability to flip a game on its head in seconds, but whom you rarely bring onto the pitch, as he doesn't fit in with the team structure. Problem-solving and investigative mathematics can undoubtedly be a real game-changer, but they are less reliable and are a riskier choice than the steadfast approach of, "Everyone follow teacher, and we'll all be fine". Problem-solving and investigative mathematics require pupils to think for themselves.

There is an interesting analogy here: great maths teachers should be nets not spoons. It's tempting and easy to stand at the front of the class doling out healthy slabs of knowledge before directing the children to answer some questions from a textbook or worksheet independently. And you may think that in doing so you've earned your custard cream at morning break. You haven't! You may even have made matters worse if you have uttered the dreaded phrase, "If you get stuck, put your hand up and I'll come and help," and in doing so have dismantled the chances of the children doing any real independent work in the lesson. Their books/sheets/mini whiteboards may be replete with answers, but you have done the majority of the thinking for them. Yes, teachers should teach, but they must also give the pupils the time and space to learn themselves.

Central to the process of weaving problem-solving into the fabric of your classroom is ensuring that you tackle the twin barriers to problem-solving: fear and lack of interest.

REDUCING THE FEAR FACTOR

The key to enthusing pupils about problem-solving is removing the main barrier that prevents independent thought, and that is fear: fear of not understanding, fear of being wrong and fear of being embarrassed. The first step to creating young problem-solvers is to reduce these fears for them. Fair enough, but how do you do this? First of all, a teacher must think carefully about how they react in the classroom when a pupil makes a mistake. A slice of perspective is crucial here. I often ask my pupils, "What's the worst that will happen?" A mistake is rarely-to-never the end of the world, and life will most certainly go on after the error.

There are many reasons why a mistake might have come about: from misinterpreting or misunderstanding the question, to applying a method incorrectly (or applying the incorrect method). But reducing the fear factor must come before trying to support any other difficulties. The kids in your class need to know that if they do not give something a go, they have a zero per cent chance of getting it right, and that even a guess is better than nothing. Once children are less fearful about making mistakes, they are more open to the idea of thinking for themselves. This all contributes to the development of, arguably, the single greatest thing that we can teach our children: resilience. Some might be uncomfortable with the idea of instilling resilience in our youngest learners, as it doesn't sound like it's going to be a very pleasant experience for either the child or the teacher. But building resilient learners is a massive part of what we are employed to do, and the fact that resilience comes through hard work and perseverance doesn't mean that it can't be developed in an incredibly fun and engaging way.

BAIT YOUR HOOK

The next step is to bait the hook with something to lure them in. The sort of problem-solving that this book seeks to promote can't be found in most textbooks. It is imaginative and it is creative, requiring the teacher to seek out problems that will inspire the pupils to find answers because they are interested, rather than because they are told to do so. This *can* seem like a daunting task – because we don't always think of mathematics as a creative subject – but it is and must be a creative subject if we are to have any chance of fostering a real interest in it. The question is, where do you get the bait from?

When I'm unsure about where to get started I go on a problem trawl. I scribble down a list of as many different problems as I can think of that I've recently encountered: ones that I've experienced, that friends have experienced, that I've read about, that I've seen on the TV. I then sift out any that would have no place in the classroom (either because they are not age appropriate or because they are boring). The ones left over are given their own piece of paper and I write down as many mathematical ideas as I can think of that could link to the problems.

I usually find that it doesn't take long before I come up with something that could potentially work. Once an idea has potential, it just needs a little tweaking and reworking to make it ready for the classroom. A steadfast formula for reworking a problem for the classroom is as follows:

(Interesting + Accessible) x Challenging = Excellent

The idea must be interesting, otherwise the children won't have any desire to work it out for themselves. It must be accessible, as the children must understand what you are talking about or be able to relate to the problem in some way. Most importantly, it must be challenging for everyone (even in a classroom with a wide range of abilities and needs). Apply the formula when you are creating classroom activities and you can't go far wrong.

This book is intended to reanimate the way that you look at primary mathematics. Its main goal is to make maths *shine*, and it aims to do so by applying the following model to everything that is contained within:

- Social. This book contains activities designed to get pupils to discuss, question and collaborate in their work. All too often, maths is taught as a lonely subject, and this book aims to address this.

- Hued. This book aims to present primary mathematics in the most colourful way possible. There are many very good vanilla teaching activities that can be used when teaching primary maths, but you won't find many of them here.

- Interlinked. This book will not present primary mathematics in discrete, easily digested nuggets of knowledge; it will challenge both teacher and learner to make links to how maths manifests in the world outside the classroom.

- **N**erve-building. This book makes no excuses for presenting ideas that may be considered to be outside of the realms of the primary curriculum. Many of the activities will challenge even the brightest primary students, but all of the activities are designed to build nerve (not nerves) by encouraging pupils to fall over and pick themselves up again.

- **E**nergetic. Put simply, this book is designed to make you move.

So ditch your spoons, grab your safety nets and let the games begin ...

Chapter 1
NUMBER

If people do not believe that mathematics is simple, it is only because they do not realize how complicated life is.

John von Neumann, keynote speech at the national meeting of the Association for Computing Machinery (1947)

I challenge anyone to live a day without using numbers. It is simply impossible to imagine a world without them, such is their integral role in everyday life. Make a list of everything you plan to do today. Would you be able to do any of them if numbers ceased to exist? The world is vastly complicated and, contrary to what some in your class/staffroom might believe, is actually made more simple by the presence of numbers. The ten little digits from 0 to 9 form the basis of a universal language that enables our world to tick ever onwards. Numbers are, therefore, inherently interesting, and a sound understanding of them unlocks almost limitless possibility. So why do some people despise them, or at least despise maths? If numbers have such incredible potential for improving our lives, why are some people indifferent towards developing their understanding of them? It is not the numbers themselves that are the problem but the uniform they're dressed up in. If numbers are the steps, then mathematics is the choreography that turns those numbers from something that your dad might light up the dance floor with at a wedding to a rhythmic masterpiece that is a pleasure to behold.

Unfortunately, the sheer amount of time that is spent on arithmetic and work on the four operations (addition, subtraction, multiplication and division) effectively kills off all interest in numbers for many individuals. Ensuring

that all children can carry out an increasingly demanding list of written calculation methods often results in there being too little time devoted to the
simple enjoyment of numbers. We have to afford ourselves a little time to
become cosier with them, to enjoy spending time in their company.

Rogerson's Book of Numbers, by Barnaby Rogerson, is a fascinating book that
delves into the role that numbers play in the arts, culture, religion and belief
systems of our world, and includes the following quote that I love: "And as
one reads it becomes clear that all our supposedly separate cultures are
magnificently interlinked and interrelated by a shared belief in the magical
significance of numbers."[1] As I read this book for the first time, I could not
help but sit in stupefied awe and fascination as I found out that Bach can
be linked by gematria (substituting numbers for letters – algebraic thinking?) to the number 14, or that the average distance between the earth and
the moon of 237,000 miles equates to 30 times the diameter of the earth!
Maybe I am a bit of an anorak here,[2] but isn't this just awesomely interesting? Rogerson's book shows just how much we should value numbers and
sets out why we should place them at the centre of what we do and what we
strive for. This is what I want my pupils to buy into. I want them to believe
that what we are doing is not only fascinating and important, but that it also
relates to who they are as a person: to what they do, what they believe and
what they want to or can achieve.

What follows in this chapter is a playful look at how we can encourage pupils
to see numbers as vastly more than just a vehicle or conduit for classroom
boredom. I have split the chapter into the basics, which you simply have to
teach, and the exciting stuff, which you simply have to teach!

---

1   Barnaby Rogerson, *Rogerson's Book of Numbers: The Culture of Numbers from 1001 Nights to
    the Seven Wonders of the World* (London: Profile, 2013).
2   Editor's note: no maybes about it.

BASICS: A, B, C AS EASY AS 1, 2, 3

Numbers are as vital to maths as letters are to English. Number recognition and counting should be the starting point for the teaching of mathematics to any child. The importance of learning to count is undeniable and, therefore, in the early years of education, a great deal of emphasis is placed on making sure the little darlings know how to get from 1 to 10 (in the correct order). However, this is just the start. The key to developing a sound understanding of numbers is not in just learning to count upwards, but in learning from an early age exactly where a number fits in relation to others. I have met many a mini-mathematician who could count upwards with complete confidence, but could not tell me what would be the third number on from 4 or what number came two places before 6 without counting on or backwards using their fingers. Initially, counting while using the fingers is fine. However, being able to count upwards from 1 to 20 is merely a rote skill; it is the same as being able to sight read words without having any comprehension of what the word means (barking at text). Children need to learn how our number system works: that you can count forwards, backwards and in steps of multiples, and that there is a specialist vocabulary related to numbers.

Counting backwards, in particular, can cause small kids real problems, and it is one of the main reasons why children encounter greater difficulty in both mental and written methods of subtraction, compared to their ability to solve addition calculations. Getting children comfortable with counting forwards, backwards and in steps is absolutely vital for building a solid foundation in arithmetic. The investment of time in developing an understanding of numbers at an early age pays off massively in the future. Even more important, though, is ensuring that we encourage pupils to be playful with numbers and to foster positive feelings about them right from the start.

Little ones should count everything: the number of steps they take, how many carrots they've eaten (or nudged around the plate), the number of leaves on a branch, the freckles on their face, the number of cracks in the pavement on the walk to school. The trouble with counting is that it gets a bit samey after a while, and the last thing we want is for them to get bored with numbers before we get on to the good stuff. So, we have to inject some life into this most basic of tasks.

Counting challenges are a good way forward. Even little learners like a challenge. The more ridiculous the counting challenge the better: how many shoes can you stack in a pile? How many items of clothing can you put on? How many tennis balls can you fit inside a hat? How many teddy bears can sit on one chair? How many pieces of spaghetti tall are you? How many grapes can you grasp in your hand? What about the other hand? Can you get more in one hand than the other? Does it matter if the grapes are red or white? Why are they called red and white when they look green and purple? It sounds silly, but it's all about sending out the right messages: being challenged can be fun; there is not just one way of doing maths; exploring different approaches pays off. And it doesn't have to be serious – counting can be a bit of a giggle.

Another simple way to develop counting skills is to play games with a pack of cards. Assign an operation to each suit: hearts mean count on one place, diamonds count on two places, spades count backwards one place and clubs count backwards two places. Shuffle the deck and place it in the centre of the table. Pupils take it in turns to turn over a card and count forwards or backwards depending on the suit. This game can be played with the whole class, with pupils split into small groups or in pairs or threes. To begin with, support the pupils by giving them a number line to work with. Once they are more comfortable with the game, you can see how quickly the pupils can work through the pack of cards, either in groups against each other or as a whole class racing against the clock to beat a previous time. You can also add in a further element of competition by dealing out the cards and setting the rule that the pupils have to answer without hesitation: the first to hesitate loses all of their cards so far (a bit like Snap) and the aim of the game is to collect all the cards in the pack. You can scale up the level of difficulty for older/more able pupils by changing the operation of each suit or assigning special properties to cards such as jokers or face cards – how about a joker doubles the current number, or a king adds 25 to the count? The versatility that a pack of cards offers to a teacher is vast, and this won't be the only time that we take a look at using cards in the classroom during the space of this book.

"WE'RE OFF TO SEE THE WIZARD ..."

For some children, counting can make them feel as if they are "a long way from Kansas, Toto".[3] This most simple of skills can cause frustration for some little ones (and even some larger ones), and it is important to make sure we have fun with it, so our pupils want to grasp it without feeling that they are being made to. I've made up a game that I love playing to help children develop their counting skills called Follow the Yellow Brick Road. First, you lay out a trail of yellow pieces of paper or card taped to the floor (the more space you have the better). The game is as simple as a PE teacher with a hangover: a step forward is a one count onwards, a step backwards is a one count backwards and a jump either forwards or backwards equals a count of a specific multiple (e.g. if a jump is set to equal 5 and the number that a child is currently on is 2, then after a jump forward they would be on 7). You can demonstrate the first round by stepping along the yellow brick road yourself, and have the class either counting along together or taking it in turns to do so. The better the pupils are, the quicker you move. Get the pupils to go along the road themselves, or vary the difficulty by adding in different multiples for the jumps and by mixing up the number that you start on (e.g. 3 rather than 1).

---

3   *The Wizard of Oz*, dir. Victor Fleming (Metro-Goldwyn-Mayer, 1939).

NOT ALL NUMBERS ARE CREATED EQUAL

In the same way that words have different properties, so do numbers. Children need to become familiar with the specific, technical language used to describe these numbers. We should encourage them to use the correct mathematical vocabulary by ensuring that we practice what we preach. First up, let's make sure we say the numbers correctly. The number 101 is one-hundred-and-one, not one-zero-one or, even worse, one-o-one. The number 3,047 is three-thousand-and-forty-seven, not three-zero-four-seven.

Saying numbers correctly, and in full, helps younger pupils with their understanding of place value. The value of each digit in our decimal number system depends on its position, or place, within a given number. Each place has a value of ten times more than the number or place immediately to the right (i.e. a digit in the tens place is worth ten times more than the same digit position in the ones). Knowing that the 3 in the thousands column is worth three thousand, and not just three, is vital. It is also important to ensure that pupils recognise the difference between 14 and 41, 63 and 36, 72 and 27. Reversal of digits and confusion over the place value of digits are common mistakes in early primary maths, but can be easily addressed by ensuring we emphasise the value of each digit in every number that we use.

Before we get on to anything else we need to talk about place value. When is a four not a four? When it is placed in any other column other than the ones column. The worst attempt at a joke ever? Nope, there is worse to come. Place value is no laughing matter though – get it wrong and children have little-to-no hope of understanding maths. A cracking way of getting children a little more pumped up about place value is to get them up on their feet for a game of Place Value Channel Hopping. This activity is best set up by giving each child a playing card at the start of the lesson or, even better, by taping it to the base of their chair to be deployed at a predetermined point. As children enter the classroom, they are greeted with a polite good morning, given a playing card and told to keep their card secret. Once all the children are sitting down with their playing card, I show them the channels I have set up at the front of the classroom, as in the example below:

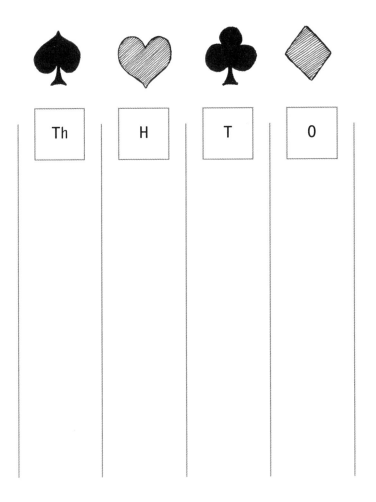

At the front of each channel is a piece of A4 card with an ace of a particular suit stuck to one side of it. Each different ace represents a different channel. I tell the pupils that they have 20 seconds to get themselves into the correct channel based on the suit of the card they were given. The children scramble to get themselves into the correct channel and, once they are there, I ask the person at the back of each line to count how many people they have in their channel, and the person at the front writes down this number on a mini whiteboard. Once all the channels have done this, I write their digits down on the board to form a four-digit number. (This could be adapted for younger children by having only two or three channels.) I ask pupils to shout out the number written down. The pupils then flip over the piece of card at the front of the line with the card attached to it. On the reverse of the card it will show the relevant abbreviation for that place value position: 'Th' for thousands, 'H' for hundreds, 'T' for tens and 'O' for ones. The children are now instructed to put their playing cards away in their pockets and ready themselves for a task that will take epic amounts of teamwork and coordination. You, the teacher, will call out numbers and the children will need to sort themselves into the appropriate channels to create the digits that make up this number.

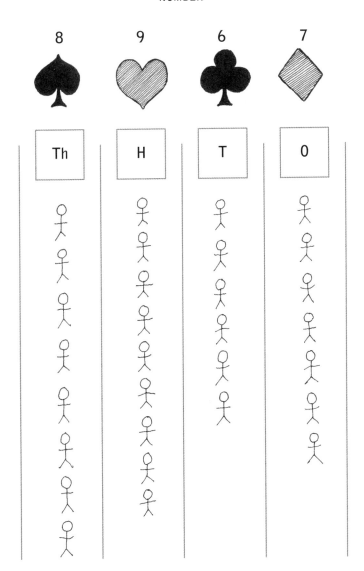

The pupils at the front of each line once again write down the digit on their mini whiteboard, so that the desired number is created in each example. This game is easily adapted to provide more fun or more urgency by changing the number of place value channels, adding in a time limit for each number, providing the desired numbers by having pupils draw them out of a hat or by using a tennis ball to act as a decimal point (more about decimals later). My personal favourite adaptation is giving them nine four-digit numbers all turned faced down on a table, along with a digital camera or phone with a camera. The pupils have to race against the clock to create all ten numbers, one after the other, ensuring that they take a photo of each number that they create. They are timed while completing the task. Once they are finished, I put the nine pictures into a square photo montage along with the time they achieved it in. I keep this posted up by the board and, every so often, give them a chance to beat their time. They love it; even shaving a couple of seconds off their time results in the class enacting a whooping celebration akin to the scoring of the winning goal in the FA Cup Final.

There are a few things to be aware of:

- There is a chance that the children will bump into each other. This can cause some teachers to worry about health and safety. Use your professional judgement here to weigh up any potential risks.

- For a class of 30, try four-digit numbers like 8967 (8 + 9 + 6 + 7 = 30) if you want all the pupils to be involved. Alternatively, start with a few examples where everyone is involved and then include numbers deliberately chosen to ensure some people will be left out. Sounds a touch cruel, but it gets the children moving more quickly.

- Make sure that you have a rule that pupils are never allowed to be at the front of a channel more than once. This avoids the movement/thinking averse child holding their spot at the front of the thousands place for the entire activity.

A slightly more sedate, though just as useful, place value activity is getting the pupils to create their own place value abacus. For this I recommend the following ingredients: plasticine or sticky tack, dried spaghetti painted different colours or different colour straws, and a pack of chocolate hoops or jelly rings.

Here is how it works:

1   Get the pupils to create a base by squishing a rectangular block of plasticine onto their desk.

2   Give them a different coloured piece of spaghetti or straw for each place on their abacus: three pieces for hundreds, tens and ones or four pieces for thousands, hundreds, tens and ones.

3   Ask the pupils to stick the spaghetti or straw upright in the plasticine fairly evenly spaced apart.

4   Pupils must then scratch the abbreviations for each place into the plasticine: 'H' for hundreds, 'T' for tens and 'O' for ones.

5   Split the cereal/sweets into different colours and ask the children to select a different colour for each place value.

6   They then thread the correct number of cereal/ sweets onto each piece of spaghetti/straw to create a visual representation of their desired number. For example, 425:

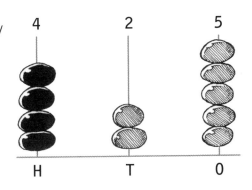

7   The children can now go around the room writing down the value illustrated on their classmates' abacuses.

Easy. Lots of questions answered, not a textbook in sight.

THAT'S ODD ...

One of the first properties of numbers that children should be introduced to is the concept of even and odd numbers. This is a relatively straightforward property to explain, as all numbers that end in 1, 3, 5, 7 or 9 are odd and those that end in 0, 2, 4, 6 or 8 are even. The real trick, though, is to ensure that pupils understand that all even numbers can be split equally in half (or between two), whereas odd numbers cannot (well, not without splitting them into parts of a whole). However, this is a touch on the dry side, and there are tons of brilliant ways that you can play with odd and even numbers. I like to pretend they are two different alien races from the planet Digiton.

Here are the Odds: Here are the Evens:

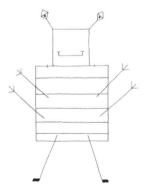

What do the children notice about these two alien races? Ask them to list all of the differences between them.

To help out, I give the children some background information about each race. The Evens are a proud, rather narcissistic bunch, who revel in their own perfection. They value symmetry (nice word) and equality above all else. They live in equal-sided square houses, and share everything equally among their friends and family. They believe in fitting in, they are neat and tidy and they strive for conformity.

The Odds are a different proposition altogether. They stand out from the crowd and believe other aliens should accept them for who they are. While some might wrongly class them as ugly, there is significant beauty in their individuality. But they are in it for themselves and don't share well with others. Despite their unruly nature, however, they are held in high regard by many, with some even being elevated to the title of 'Prime'. In spite of their clear differences, the Odds and Evens live harmoniously and often families can be comprised of both Odds and Evens. Odds and Evens will readily multiply with each other, and if an Odd and an Even have a child together they always produce offspring that are Evens. These two very different races have one thing in common, and that is that in both cases the last digit of the number, like a surname, denotes whether they are an Odd or an Even.

This may seem like a long-winded way of introducing a fairly easy concept, but consider how rich this context could be for an emerging mathematician. The vocabulary and concepts that are touched on within this idea extend far beyond the basics and, although not all children will be able to grasp the full range of concepts at first, you have sown a significant seed.

Following this introduction to the Odds and Evens, I get the kids to create their own Odds and Evens out of coloured card before attaching them to wooden lollipop sticks. I then project a series of numbers onto the board and ask the pupils to raise the appropriate lollipop stick based on whether the number is an Odd or an Even. This reinforces the importance of the last digit being the deciding factor in whether a number is odd or even.

I then like to linger on the notion of symmetry and equivalence. I get children to draw a line down the middle of an Even I have doodled earlier, and we discuss how it is the same on each side of the dividing line: it is equal.

Ask the children to try this with an Odd. What do they notice? This reinforces the fact that all even numbers can be split in half equally, whereas odd numbers cannot. But what does equals mean?

= EQUALS ANSWER, RIGHT?

What do we use the equals symbol to show? If you are being truly honest, more than half of the people reading this book would have said "the answer". However, in true Ronseal style, this symbol does exactly what it says on the tin: namely, it shows that things are equal. However, lots of children seem to miss out on this important information, instead believing that the equals sign is like a pointer that directs the reader to the answer. It might seem like I'm splitting hairs here, but it's an important distinction.

First, when we take = as meaning the answer, we are assuming that there is only one answer to a calculation. At this point, many of you will be muttering to yourselves that there is only one answer! It's maths after all: it is either right or it is wrong. 2 + 2 always = 4, always has done and always will do. Except that isn't the only solution – what about 2 + 2 = 2 x 2, or 2 + 2 = 10 – 6, or 2 + 2 = 44 ÷ 11? Are these not all appropriate answers? It appears that there are, indeed, many more ways than one to skin a cat.

ANYONE CAN FEED STEAK TO CROCODILES

A second issue with = simply signifying "here comes the answer" is that we are pushing the idea to kids that, in order to have a complete calculation, we must always use an equals sign. Not necessarily true. For a start, we have these guys: < and >, the inequality signs of less than and greater than. In the primary education world these are often known as crocodile signs. I remember being taught about them as crocodiles when I was little, and the analogy is still used today. It is a great analogy, but it is often used a little too half-heartedly for my liking. We have a great concept here begging for a bucket of WOW! to be poured all over it. So, the first thing we do is put some flesh on the bones.

I set the scene in the zoo: where Chunky the Greedy Crocodile is weighing up the menu choices for his evening meal. Should he have the contents of food bowl 1, seven juicy steaks? Or the contents of bowl 2, nine juicy steaks? The children vote and almost unanimously go for bowl 2. When asked to justify their answer, they tend to go for reasons along the lines of him getting more steak in bowl 2. We find out that he does, indeed, choose bowl 2 and, in fact, always chooses the bowl with the most food in it. He is an incredibly greedy crocodile, but at least he is consistent, always opening his jaws for the largest portion of food: the biggest amount.

At this point, the children use a laminated drawing of an open-jawed Chunky the Croc to decide between several pairs of food portions, following the rule that Chunky will always point his gaping mouth towards the biggest amount. After the children have had a chance to have a go at some examples themselves, I get them to try to describe in words the relationship between the two amounts using a set of missing gap sentences – for example, "3 is _____ than 5 or 7 is _____ than 2." We are looking for the words *less than* and *greater than*, but other suggestions are just as valuable. Once we have got the vocabulary sorted, we can really have some fun with inequalities(!).

CHUNKY THE CROC

How to create a Chunky the Croc hat

1 Get your hands on some shoeboxes. (Clarks shoe boxes are perfect for this as they are already an appealing shade of green and this therefore saves you time as you don't have to paint them.)

2 Get the children to cut jagged teeth along the joining edges of the lid and base of the box.

3 Attach masking tape to join the lid and base along one short end so that will open and close like a pair of jaws.

4 It is then up to the children to draw or stick the details on their crocodiles, such as the scales, eyes and nostrils.

If I have enough crocodile hats to go around, I split the children into groups of three. Two children play the role of zookeeper and the third plays the role of the croc. The two zookeepers need a mini whiteboard or a sheet of paper to write on, and the croc needs to put on the croc hat. The two zookeepers position themselves on either side of the croc. Both zookeepers write down a number (I tend to give the children some parameters to work within, e.g. numbers below 50) on their mini whiteboard and keep it hidden, for the time being, from the croc. When both zookeepers have written down their number they count down from 3, 2, 1 … and reveal their numbers to the croc. The croc then has to decide which amount he wants to point his open jaws at and gobble up. When the croc has decided, he or she shouts out the decision as a number sentence – for example, "Three is less than 16." Pupils can have a few goes and then swap around so everyone gets a chance to be the croc. Once settled into the task, try setting the crocs the challenge of completing five examples in 30 seconds.

I'VE GOT LESS THAN NOTHING!

Here is a conversation between two 9-year-old pupils in one of my classes who were putting numbers into order on a 'washing line'.

Dan: My number is the lowest number, so it needs to go at the end. Right here.

Maisie: Mine is lower, though, because it has a minus sign in front of it. That means it is a minus number, so it's lower than yours. Move your one up a bit.

Dan: No, mine is a zero. It's the lowest number. You can't get lower than zero.

Maisie: Yes, you can. You can have minus numbers like my one.

Dan: But your number has 14 on it. Mine is zero, it's nothing. How can you have less than nothing?

Maisie: I don't know, you just can and mine is lower. So move your one.

How is it possible to have less than nothing? Dan is not the first person to have thought that exact thing. In fact, I remember thinking this same thought a great deal during my years at university, where I would have given anything to have nothing as, in reality, I had far less. The concept of numbers that go below zero is not an easy one to comprehend initially. Before we delve into the realms of negative numbers, let's have a little look at the gatekeeper of zero itself, as it has a fair amount to answer for.

The main issue with zero is its relationship with the word 'nothing', at least in terms of language. Zero has no value, but it is not nothing (to coin a double negative). It is decidedly something. Although 0 is a number in its own right, it is often at its most useful when acting as a placeholder. I sometimes like to think of it as a form of mathematical punctuation. Without punctuation, words do not form a sentence and don't make much sense. The same can be said of zero in that it allows numbers to make sense. Eight-hundred-and-five would be written as 85 without the zero, and one-thousand-and-one would be 11 if both zeros were missing. The trouble is that kids, particularly when they are just starting to write their calculations in a formal way, leave out a zero here and a zero there thinking nothing of it: it's only a zero, after all. A teacher's job here is to make sure that missing out zeros is seen as the worst possible of all maths crimes, and should be punishable by being made to eat a bucket of Brussels sprouts while listening to Coldplay.

Back to Dan and Maisie. There really is no need to be negative about negative numbers, as they are not that difficult, at least to begin with, and can be quite good fun. The basic stumbling block with negative numbers is that a negative number that appears higher is in fact worth less. For example, 14 is a higher number than 7 so -14 appears initially as if it should be worth more than -7, but it is, in fact, worth less. This is not too much of a hurdle to negotiate, though, you just need to contextualise the issue a little.

The concept of having less than nothing is quite difficult to imagine, but when placed on a scale it becomes easier to understand. Counting along horizontal number lines is a standard way of reinforcing this concept and they can be used to good effect, especially if you incorporate a game of Follow the Yellow Brick Road (described earlier in this chapter). However, I feel that negative numbers are explained even more effectively through the use of a vertical number line. What's more, this vertical number line is even more effective when tweaked a little. Negative numbers can be explained well through the metaphorical context of being underground or underwater. You can superimpose your number line on a picture of the ocean:

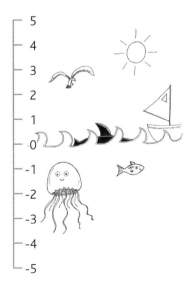

Or a forest:

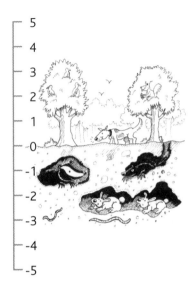

Or even a hotel with a lift running through the middle:

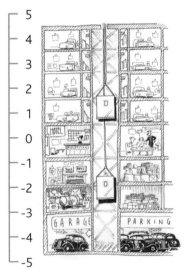

You then have incredible contexts for exploring negative numbers.

Negative numbers become really fun when you start to add and subtract with them. This can be somewhat confusing for the children at first, but remind them of the following rules and they can't go wrong:

- Add a positive number – the value increases.

- Minus a positive number – the value decreases.

- Add a negative number – the value decreases.

- Minus a negative number – the value increases.

The context of going to the bank is great for reinforcing this, as is the idea that adding money (positive) to your account makes your balance go up and adding debt (negative) to your account makes your balance go down. Children can have a lot of fun playing bank manager but, given the role of education in reinforcing moral values, I'm not entirely sure that we should be training them too heavily in the art of financial exploitation.

BEING PART OF SOMETHING

I love pizza but I hate fractions. Now fractions are starting to make me hate pizza.

Rachel

Don't do it. Resist the temptation to reach for the cardboard/laminated pizza slices. It's not that this isn't a valid teaching activity, far from it, in fact. It's just that if you teach upper Key Stage 2, the children have no doubt encountered this ubiquitous attempt at explaining fractions countless times before, and it smacks of can't be bothered. If you are going to use pizza, get a real one!

Fractions, decimals and percentages have a reputation for being tough to understand, posing a barrier for many primary (and much older) pupils. However, they are types of numbers to do with parts of something, and this concept is represented around us in countless ways.

Fractions of shapes

The easiest representation of fractions is as parts of a shape or object. The work that you put in at this stage is vital for embedding a level of understanding that goes beyond the superficial recognition of what a half, a third or a quarter look like.

Before troubling them with written representations, children should get confident in using the words 'quarter', 'half' and 'fraction' as being parts of one. Notice that I have used the term 'part of one' and not 'part of a whole'. The reason for using one rather than whole is to reduce confusion later on when ordering mixed numbers – for example, we say 'one-and-a-half' not 'whole-and-a-half', or 'three-and-three-quarters' not 'three-wholes-and-three-quarters'. Fractions are confusing enough without us presenting our learners with sloppy mathematical language!

Two identical balls of string and a pair of scissors provide the perfect tools for a fantastic introduction to fractions. Take one of the balls of string and cut it into pieces to be shared among the class. You have to be a bit clever with your cutting because you want to end up with one piece of string that is 1 m long, two pieces that are 50 cm long, four pieces that are 25 cm long and two pieces that are around 45 cm long. The remaining string can be cut up into a variety of lengths to suit the number of pupils in your class. With the amount of cutting required this is best done in advance, rather than on the fly.

Each child is then given a piece of string and asked to order themselves from shortest piece to longest piece. Once they are in order, I show them a metre ruler and ask if anyone has a piece of string that they think is the same (equivalent) length as the ruler. Once we have found the child with the piece of string that is a metre long, we introduce the word 'half'. Often children have heard this word before but require clarification on what it means. I highlight where the halfway point is on the metre ruler using a gold star or something similar to provide a visual cue. I ask the children if anyone has a piece of string that is half the length of the metre piece. Hopefully, at least four of the children will step forward and, ideally, they will be the two children with 50 cm lengths and the two children with 45 cm lengths. Make sure that the pupils notice the difference between the two pieces that are *nearly* half and the two that are actually half. Ask the children whether this matters; after all, the two 45 cm pieces of string are very close indeed to the 50 cm pieces. Show them what happens if you put the two pieces of 45 cm together compared to the two 50 cm pieces against the metre ruler. Are they the same? Show them clearly that the two pieces of string that are 50 cm long are equivalent to the 1 m piece when laid end to end, but the other two are not. There will be some pupils who won't see why this important, at which point offering two children a strawberry lace split into two unequal lengths should underline why two *halves* of the same object must be the same size or amount.

If you want to extend the children further, you could identify the four pieces of string that are 25 cm long as quarters, although this will depend on their understanding or prior knowledge. Don't rush it. You can always come back to the string in another lesson to introduce quarters.

Finally, I ask the pupils to lay all of their pieces of string end to end.[4] We then unravel the second ball of string alongside the pieces that the children have laid end to end. If your cutting was careful then you should have two long pieces of string that are the same length. Explain that the two balls of string are the same, but that one ball of string was cut up into pieces to share among the class, and that we call these parts fractions. Explain that when all of the fractions of a whole are added together they are the same as the whole.

This activity leads nicely into giving the pupils opportunities to halve other objects. Physical representations of fractions are vital in the beginning and the more things that the kids can cut, rip, spilt, tear, share or divide the better. Give them the opportunity to split the objects in different ways: give them modelling clay and cotton wool to pull apart with their hands, bananas, cakes and sandwiches to cut with a (blunt) plastic knife, dried spaghetti to snap, jugs of water to pour, paper to fold and tear, and pieces of string to snip with scissors. Avoid using solid objects that are already comprised of several pieces (e.g. a bag of sweets or Multi-Link cubes), as these can create further confusion in the early stages. For example, if I have a tower of Multi-Link cubes that is ten Multi-Link cubes tall and I halve it, am I halving 10 or halving 1? Remember, children must understand the concept of halving an object or shape before progressing on to halving quantities.

Once the pupils have worked their way through splitting their given objects in half, ask them how they can be sure that they have split the objects in half. You are looking to reinforce the vital concept that two halves of an object must be equal to the whole. Ask them to think of ways that they could check whether their halves are actually halves. It is very difficult to divide something equally in half without having something to gauge your measurements against. Provide them with scales, rulers, tape measures and measuring jugs to assess the splitting they have already done and ask them

---

4   You will need a decent amount of space for this depending on the size of the ball of string.

to suggest how they could have improved on their work. The conceptual understanding of splitting things equally does not come easily to all and should not be rushed. Give it time. Remember, the importance of sharing sweets equally with sharks. Only when pupils can physically divide objects into both halves and quarters do I move on.

The next stage is to move on to more abstract examples of splitting objects into fractions. For this we need shapes. In the first instance, we want to look at shapes that the children are already comfortable with, that are regular and easily measured. For this reason rectangles (including squares[5]) are brilliant; even more so when they are presented cut out on squared paper as this allows for easy measuring without the need for rulers. Give pupils rectangles of different sizes and proportions.

First, ask them to divide the rectangles in half by drawing a line with a ruler through the centre of the rectangle and then shading one half with a coloured pencil. Compare the work from different pupils to show that there is more than one way to halve a rectangle, with lines going both vertically and horizontally through the centre point. Reinforce the concept of equivalence by getting the children to fold their shapes along the line they have drawn. Show the pupils examples of rectangles which have not been divided through the middle and ask them to explain how they can tell that it has not been split in half. As an extension, show them how to draw a diagonal line through the rectangle. Ask the pupils whether the shape has been split in half. The class will often be divided in their opinion,[6] as the two fractions of the shape look the same size but when folded they do not lie flat on top of each other. By asking the pupils to cut down the diagonal line, they can then place the two halves on top of each other to show that they are equivalent.

---

5   Yes, a square is a rectangle, but a rectangle is not necessarily a square.
6   Pun may or may not be intended.

Once the halving and quartering of objects and shapes is secure, it is time to move on to teaching the basics of fractions of quantity. When moving into fractions of quantity, transition using what the children already know. Regular shapes with representations of numbers contained within them are the order of the day. Chocolate bars are great for the following activity:

1   Provide pairs of pupils with a chocolate bar and ask them to count how many pieces of chocolate there are in the whole chocolate bar.

2   Ask them to split the bar in half so that they each get the same number of pieces.

3   Ask them to count the number of pieces in their half and the number of pieces in their partner's half. Reinforce that they can only be halves if they each have the same number of pieces.

4   Ask the pupils to split their halves in half again and to count the number of pieces they now have in each of their two piles. Ask them what they split their half into, with the aim of eliciting two quarters. Reinforce the point that two quarters are equivalent to one half. Emphasise that if they put all of their quarters together they are equivalent to one whole chocolate bar.

5   Optional.[7] Pupils place a quarter of a chocolate bar each in their gobs and munch away happily. Reserve the remaining chocolate as a 'carrot' for the remainder of the lesson/day.

Next, I bring the children back together to show them a larger chocolate bar. We count how many pieces there are in the bar and discuss how this differs from the smaller chocolate bars they were given. We then split the big bar in half and count the number of pieces in each half. I ask the children if this can be half a chocolate bar if it has a different number of pieces in it to the

---

7   Not the healthiest option, but they will be putty in your hands for the rest of the lesson!

halves that they got from their chocolate bars. I explain that, just like when we split shapes or objects of different proportions in half, we get halves of different amounts from different wholes and that the important thing is that both halves of a whole are equal in amount.

I then show the children a set of Multi-Link cubes and repeat the process to show that the concepts we have just covered do not apply solely to chocolate bars. I finish by showing them a range of rectangles on squared paper with lines drawn through to split them into halves and quarters. Having already experienced splitting rectangles into halves and quarters, the children are asked to count the number of squares that are present in each half and then in each quarter. I then show them a rectangle which has been split into two sections, but instead of a straight line drawn through the centre of the shape, I have drawn a jagged line, like so:

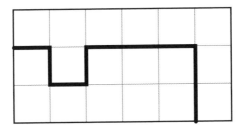

I then get the pupils to discuss whether this rectangle has been split in half or not. Most tend to think not because it doesn't look like any half that they have seen before. I ask the pupils how we could check. We count the squares and find out that it is, indeed, split in half because there are, say, nine squares in one half and nine in the other half. I then set the pupils a challenge to see how many different ways they could split this rectangle in half by drawing different lines through the shape. This can then be repeated with quarters.

The children love this activity because no matter how many ways they find of dividing the rectangle in half, they always seem to find another way.[8]

Once they are in Year 2, pupils are expected to begin to write fractions in a formal way, with one number over another. This can be daunting and confusing for some, so it is important to reinforce what they already know about fractions and then to lay down some ground rules.

Fractions have awesome vocabulary: numerator, denominator and, my favourite, vinculum. These words sound proper mathsy, which is a good thing. Despite their occasional protestations, children love things which are perceived as difficult. Saying numerator instead of top number is not a great deal more difficult, but it gives the impression of proper mathematical boffinicity. All this means that the children feel more chuffed with themselves when they master it.[9]

Fractions are created by splitting a whole thing into several pieces. The total number of pieces is written on the bottom and is called the *denominator*. Make links between denominator and denominations.

Once an object has been split into a number of pieces it can be shared out. How the total number of pieces is shared can vary: one person could receive more pieces than another and the number of people that the pieces are shared among can also vary. The number of pieces that you are focusing on at any given time is called the *numerator*, and it is written on top of the denominator.

---

8   How many ways can you find?
9   Try playing *Call my Bluff* with mathematical vocabulary – for example: Is a vinculum (a) a creature that lives in the reception sandpit and only comes out at night, (b) a tool for making straight lines out of circles, (c) a horizontal line that separates the numerator and denominator when writing fractions or (d) the fancy name for earwax?

The thing that keeps the numerator and the denominator separate is the *vinculum*; this is a horizontal line that acts as a helpful indicator that splitting and sharing has taken place.

At this stage, pupils are also introduced to a wider range of fractions, including thirds and non-unit fractions in the form of quarters. They are also expected to be able to count in fractional steps up to and beyond 1 (e.g. $\frac{1}{4}$, $\frac{2}{4}$, $\frac{1}{2}$), $\frac{3}{4}$, 1, 1 $\frac{1}{4}$, 1 $\frac{1}{2}$, 1 $\frac{3}{4}$). I use a simple counting line game to reinforce this called Adam the Apple Hunter. It's easy to set up: all you need is a bag of apples which have been cut into quarters and placed on plates that are positioned at intervals of a quarter on a long number line across either the floor or a set of tables. This activity can be carried out in small groups or as a whole class with children taking it in turns to be Adam and stepping along the number line collecting quarters of apple as they go. Once four quarters have been collected, these are put together to form a whole apple and the count continues. Once they get good at this game, you can get them stepping forwards or backwards; and if they are really good, in steps that cover more than one quarter at a time. Tenths are the next fraction to be introduced, and this brings the start of exploring decimal numbers. It is important for the children to see that 0.1 is equivalent to 1 ÷ 10 right from the beginning of their learning of tenths, as this helps to reinforce that decimal numbers and fractions are both ways of representing parts of something.

Once we get into Year 4, we are into the good stuff. It is at this stage that children should not only be working with a range of fractions but also decimal numbers in the form of hundredths. This is where the idea of equivalence – not just between fractions but also between fractions, decimals and even the beginnings of percentages – comes into play. The key to all of this is reinforcing the idea that fractions, decimals and percentages are all just numbers that represent part of something.

In my experience, there is one resource that reigns supreme in the quest for concrete fraction, decimal and percentage understanding: the hundred square (grid). If you have any spare space in your playground, one of the best things you can do is draw a large 10 x 10 grid, ideally with 1 m² squares, on the floor in chalk or paint. This is an invaluable resource which can be used for all manner of maths related activities, from counting games, to times tables, to plotting shapes and graphs, to what we will use it for in this instance: demonstrating 100 parts of a whole. The first time that I use the giant hundred square for fractions, decimals and percentages, I place 25 items on the grid, one in each square, grouped together to cover a quarter of the grid. The items can be anything that you like but I tend to use sports equipment like footballs or cones.

The first question that I ask the children is, "What fraction of this grid has got an object in it?" As the children have already covered quarters, they usually get this straightaway. Next, I ask them, "What fraction of the grid is covered using an equivalent fraction to ¼?" Once we have got the answer $^{25}/_{100}$, I ask them if there is another way that we could write this that is not a fraction. We recap on decimal numbers and look at how we could write $^{25}/_{100}$ as a decimal number. Once we understand that 25 objects out of a possible 100 can be written as both $^{25}/_{100}$ and 0.25, we can have all sorts of fun with our grid. You can get the pupils to place more or less objects on the grid to give them different fractions and decimals. They can explore equivalent fractions and other representations of 100 parts of a whole, such as 100 pennies equalling a pound. You can even begin to start introducing percentages, which is not much of a leap considering that that they have already been playing with fractions that have 100 as the denominator.

The work that comes in the latter stages of the primary curriculum to do with fractions, decimals and percentages centres around calculations, but all of the groundwork that you put in during the earlier stages will pay massive dividends when the children get on to the number crunching at a later stage.

DANCING ABOUT ALGEBRA

What does the Little Mermaid wear to cover her modesty?

An algae-bra.

When many people think of difficult maths, they probably think of an incomprehensible calculation involving a lot of funny looking brackets and letters where normally numbers would be. The average primary school teacher may view the idea of teaching their little ones algebra as yet another ridiculous demand being placed on them by people who know nothing about teaching ("What will I be expected to teach them next, open-heart surgery?!") and the average primary aged child might be reduced to tears by a page full of a's and b's when they were expecting 1's and 2's. However, the beauty of it is in its difficulty: because it is perceived as being so hard, when you actually manage to crack it in the classroom – whether as a primary teacher or as a primary pupil – you feel very chuffed indeed with yourself. Harness the fact that algebra has a tough reputation: let the children believe that they are incredible mathematicians because they have cracked algebra! You don't have to let anyone know it's actually a complete doddle. Keep that to yourself and bask in the reflected glory that comes with your class being master mathematicians.

At its most basic level, algebra is about using symbols to signify unknown quantities – for example, $a + b = c$ for $1 + 2 = 3$. This replacing of numbers with letters is often referred to as 'substitution', in that a number has been substituted by a letter. This is not a difficult concept to grasp. To reduce the fear factor, I suggest asking the kids to do some of their own substituting by replacing the digits from 0 to 9. There are three ways I would recommend doing this:

1   Get the children to assign a colour to each digit (mildly boring).

2   Ask the children to draw or use a font such as Wingdings to create their own symbols for each digit (mildly enjoyable).

3   Make up dance moves for each digit (the next level of enjoyment, comparable only in intensity to eating white chocolate).

Assuming that you make the right choice and go for option 3, here are a few pointers to help out:

- Pupils will always perform better at this sort of thing when working in pairs or threes. Make sure that you take the lead in selecting the groups. Contrary to what Ben might think, you know who works most effectively together.

- Give pupils time to prepare. Don't rush them through this sort of task, as activities that require creativity from pupils can fall flat on their face if you do not give them sufficient time to prepare. This is especially true if you are going to ask the children to demonstrate their work to the rest of the class. Kids want the opportunity to shine, not to be embarrassed in front of their mates.

- This works better in a hall or somewhere with plenty of space to move around. If this is not possible, then make sure all desks and/or tripping hazards have been moved to the sides of the room.

If you are expecting the kids to do this, then you must be prepared to give it a go too. Prepare one yourself and use it as an icebreaker by going first before the pupils, offer to accompany any groups who are a bit nervous or, if you are something of a Travolta, offer to show your moves as a grand finale to the lesson. Remember that you are the benchmark: if you are reserved, dull and nervous, the children may well behave in a similar way.

Once they have sorted their alternative 0 to 9's, the pupils should demo their moves in front of the rest of the class. For maximum effect and amusement,

I give children access to a playlist of tracks that they can use to accompany their routine. This is an activity guaranteed to bring a smile to the face of anyone in the classroom, including, on one occasion, a rather grumpy looking observer who was not quite sure what to make of it all until, just as Gloria Estefan promised, the rhythm did indeed get him (even box-tickers can boogie)!

This initial foray into the algebraic boogie is simply the start. The next step is for the class to experiment with creating their own equations using the dance moves they have devised. This is simply done. First, to get pupils used to the idea, give them a few simple arithmetic questions to translate into dance (e.g. 4 + 3 = 7 or 5 − 2 = 3). One suggestion is that, when creating these calculations, the pupils shout out which operation they are doing, as well as the word 'equals' before their answer to reduce potential for confusion – for example, "Dad wedding shuffle *plus* stack the shelves *equals* zombie move out of *Thriller*," or "Running man *minus* cowboy gunslinger *equals* Slash-esque knee-slide."

Once they have spent a few minutes substituting the digits in simple calculations using their dance moves, get pupils to create their own simple equations using them. They create a simple equation, which their partner then solves before having a go at creating their own equation. When you feel that it's time to move on, the next step is to get the pupils to create short pieces of choreography that act as 'missing gap' calculations. The idea is that each pair or group creates a series of three calculations that contain missing gaps in the information – for example, move A + move B = 7, move A − 2 = 3 or move B x 4 = 8. Therefore, move A = 5 and move B = 2.

When we look at algebra we have to realise one thing pretty quickly, and that is that we may not be able to answer an algebraic equation quite so quickly: it may take more than one step. In the example above, we can come up with several suggestions for what move A and move B could equal. But, until we have carried out and seen our further examples, we cannot be sure of both values. This idea can be adapted easily in any number of ways, from children using glove puppets instead of dance moves to varying what they *must* and *must not* include in their calculations. Just remember that children are creatures of habit and, unless we take them out of their comfort zone where, even for a moment, there could be more than one right answer, they will always expect maths to remain a black and white subject.

FUNCTION MACHINES

Another cracking way of developing algebraic thinking is to take a look at function machines. Function machines work on the premise that you add an input, and then either a function or a rule alters the input number to give an output.

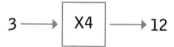

In the above example, if we add 3 as an input, it gets multiplied by 4 and therefore the output is 12. If we used 7 as an input we would get an answer of 28, if the function remained the same (i.e. input multiplied by 4). Function machines are often introduced to children with the functions on display, but I think this takes all of the fun out of them. The beauty of function machines is that they promote investigatory thought as children seek to obtain an answer through trial, error and investigation. With the functions hidden, you cannot be certain of what the function is until you have tried several different input numbers.

In the function machine above, we can see that when we pass 7 through the machine we get 21. The function could be multiply by 3, but it could also be add 14. We can only be sure once we have tried another input number. This process is the absolute pinnacle of what primary maths should be about: valuing the process above the answer.

Function machines are often presented in textbooks as an array of different coloured and shaped boxes with an assortment of different arrows to illustrate that there is a process going on. Sometimes there are illustrations of robots or (hold on to your chair ...) mechanical elements such as cogs or levers! Oh, the unbridled excitement! Not convinced? Neither am I. Function machines cannot be done justice through the medium of textbook or worksheet. They need to be whizzing, whirring and whooshing machines if they are to really grab our pupils' attention.

This is a standard illustration of a function machine that you can find in most textbooks or worksheets that cover the topic:

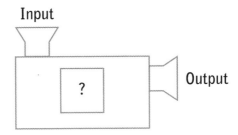

Pretty straightforward: it ultimately consists of something going in a box (input), in which something happens (functions) and, finally, something that comes out (output). Bearing this in mind, it becomes quickly apparent that it wouldn't take much to transform this into a physical reality. Enter the FUNctionator-3000.

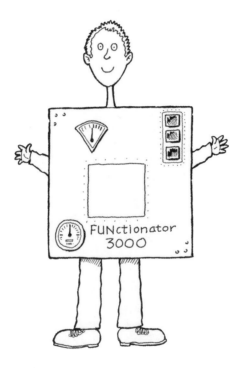

A large cardboard box (big enough to disappear inside of) and several rolls of tin foil are all you need to get started. Of course, you can make your FUNctionator as complex or as basic as you like. (I usually add flared sides to put my arms through which emphasises the input and output parts of the machine, and cut a door flap at stomach level on the front of the box, as this allows me to attach a mini whiteboard to the reverse side on which I write the function.)

Kids love playing in cardboard boxes. Forget iPads! The simple pleasure gained from messing about in a cardboard box is unbeatable. To deploy the FUNctionator most effectively, I suggest setting the scene by turning the classroom lights off, playing some robot sound effects or some suitable electronic music (almost anything by Justice works well for this), before entering the classroom inside your FUNctionator-3000. Explain that the FUNctionator is an advanced arithmetic machine sent back from the future with a mission to enhance mathematical understanding in the young of today to avoid a future world crisis.

For the whole class teaching aspect of it, I tend to write down a function on the mini whiteboard inside the FUNctionator before asking a pupil to write down a single digit number on a sticky note. This note is read out to the class before being passed to me through the input slot on the FUNctionator. I then pop my head and arms inside the confines of the box and write down what the output is on the reverse of the sticky note that acted as the input. While I'm working inside the box, the pupils make an assortment of their best possible mechanical noises until I suddenly pop my head and arms out of the box with a ping. At this point, the pupils get ready to catch the output, which is thrown out of the output hole. The pupil who catches the sticky note reads the output to the rest of the class, and all the pupils jot down the possibilities that the function could be. The pupils then discuss what would be a good number to put through the FUNctionator next.

We repeat the process with a second input number. Once the second output is read out, many of the pupils will work out what the function is, but I always get them to put through at least one more number, so they can check they are absolutely correct. When the class have agreed on what they think the function is, I pop open the mini whiteboard door on the front of the FUNctionator to reveal the answer.

Following this initial FUNctionator episode, I get the kids to create their own mini function machines in groups. Assorted junk, including cardboard boxes, kitchen roll tubes, paper cups and copious amounts of tin foil, is needed in vast quantities for this. A tried and tested design is as follows:

1   Grab a copier paper box and cut down the back wall on both edges from top to bottom to create a flap.

2   Create a reusable surface for writing the function on by taping a laminating sheet to the inside of the cardboard flap.

3   Cut off the base of two paper cups and, using the base as a template, cut a paper cup sized hole in the top of the box, on the right hand side, about halfway up.

4   Insert the cups into the holes in the box to create input and output funnels.

5   Decorate as you wish.

Once the pupils have their own function machines, they can take it turns in their group to repeat the first learning episode with them cast in the role of teacher. I have yet to meet a child who hasn't enjoyed this activity, and they will quite happily work through a huge amount of examples without even noticing how hard they are working. A classroom full of giggling children, all trying to do their best robot noises, while working their socks off, is an incredibly gratifying sight, and one I don't think I will ever tire of.

The next step is to introduce the idea of multiple functions, which increases the level of challenge quite significantly. However, because the pupils have become so confident in what they are doing by this point, they will happily tackle it head on. Line up two of the mini function machines they have created next to each other, pass an input number through the first machine, then through the second, before revealing the output. The range of possible functions is considerably increased and the pupils will need to carefully consider and discuss what input to pass through the machine next if they are to trial their theories effectively. If they are struggling, I might give them a clue by letting them know what the output is after the first machine, before passing it through the second. Practise your robot moves, give it a go and I guarantee you will enjoy it as much as the children do!

If all that talk of 'crafts' makes you uncomfortable then there are other ways of avoiding rubbishy, boring worksheets. There are some cracking function machine simulations online – I rate these two particularly highly:

- http://www.amblesideprimary.com/ambleweb/mentalmaths/function-machines.html

- http://www.mathplayground.com/functionmachine.html

Function machines are a phenomenal way to encourage children to trial and improve their work. This is not a black and white activity; it offers children the opportunity to value their mistakes as an intrinsic part of the process of getting to the correct answer. I hope that you can see why I love function machines and how, with a little bit of tinfoil, your pupils will love them too.

THE GOOD STUFF

As I alluded to in the introduction to this book, maths was distinctly uninteresting to me throughout my education from primary school to teacher training. On the one hand, I don't think I really gave it a fair chance – probably because it was difficult and there were other things that came far easier to me. On the other hand, I don't think that I was ever exposed to sufficiently exciting concepts or ideas to make me stop and go WOW! I was never hooked in by it. If I were a betting man (and I bet you are), I would wager a small handful of beans that I'm not alone among primary practitioners in this feeling. Part of the problem is that we are all so concerned with ensuring that our pupils grasp the basics that we have neither the time nor the inclination to introduce them to mathematical concepts that truly knock their socks off. These mathematical concepts get left until the latter stages of mathematics education, by which point you have already developed a Marmite feeling towards the subject.

I believe that we shouldn't shy away from throwing difficult and complex mathematical concepts at our primary pupils. I'm sure many think something along the lines of, "But you have be able to walk before you can run." I would agree with you to a point; however, I think that we tend to not only strive for our children to walk the mathematical walk, but also for them to march it in perfect synchronisation too, so that our approach to maths looks like something dreamt up in a command HQ somewhere in deepest Pyongyang. What if, yes, we concerned ourselves with getting children comfortable on their mathematical feet, but instead of forcing them to march with the knowledge, we asked them to hop, skip, dance, stumble, trip and, on occasions, fall too?

I was a fairly uncoordinated though adventurous child. I climbed things I probably shouldn't have climbed and threw myself off things I shouldn't have thrown myself off with gusto. I hurt myself a lot, almost becoming on first name terms with the nurses in Ipswich Hospital A&E. I had bloody good fun doing it though. What's more, I still want to climb things. What if we approached constructing children's experiences with numbers in a similar vein, making space for concepts that foster 'Ooooooos' rather than 'Ohs'. Let's worry less about what attainment level young children are 'working at', and concern ourselves more with what interest level they are 'working at'. In the same way that we push intervention to support our pupils to make necessary academic progress in line with their peers, I suggest that we also push intervention that addresses a lack of interest in maths and numbers.

In order to achieve this successfully, we need to offer our pupils a banquet of numerical delicacies that they don't usually get to taste, such is the bland and beige nature of a regular mathematical diet. What follows is a suggested menu of numerical *amuse-bouches* to be served to hungry primary punters: base number broth, mathemagical surprise and a slice of Pascal's triangle.

BASE NUMBER BROTH

If I asked you to write out the number sixteen in digits you would find it easy, right? What about if I asked you to write it out in Roman numerals? Or how about binary? I would hazard a guess that there would be a few furrowed brows, and can guarantee that there would be a few more if you asked your classes to do this. But why would you not ask them to do it? A while back, I had a discussion with a teacher at another school about the changes to the primary maths curriculum (life doesn't get much more exciting!), and I was interested to hear that she thought that the introduction of Roman numerals into the suggested Year 3 programme of study was a waste of time. Her justification was that we count using a decimal system and have no need to teach children a useless number system they will never use.

While not wanting to get too side-tracked into a wider debate about what is and isn't useful, I felt disappointed for her. For a start, Roman numerals are still used today, albeit infrequently, and children should know what all those X's and I's equate to. More importantly, though, looking at Roman numerals, or any other number system, is a chance to take children out of their comfort zone and break some of those all too familiar rules that we have spent ages drumming into them. In short, it will enable them to think about numbers with greater flexibility and, hopefully, with renewed interest too.

Roman numerals are made up of several letters from the Latin alphabet. Although in ancient Rome the exact usage of symbols would have varied, the seven symbols used today are as follows:

Symbol	Value
I	1
V	5
X	10
L	50
C	100
D	500
M	1,000

Numbers are formed by placing symbols next to each other and adding their values together (e.g. II: 1 + 1 = 2, VI: 5 + 1 = 6). This is all pretty straightforward. The only bit where it becomes tricky is the fact that the Romans must have not cared much for the idea of writing four of the same symbol next to each to other. Therefore, instead of writing IIII for four or LXXXX for 90, they came up with a nifty idea to counteract their fear of four. By placing a I before V or X, the numerals for 4 and 9 are created by subtracting one from 5 and 10. This system is also applied with X being placed before L and C to create 40 and 90, as well as with C being placed before D and M to create 400 and 900. An example of this could be the year this book was written, 2014, which would be written as MMXIV (not MMXIIII).

So, what are you going to do with Roman numerals? Well, the easy option would be to give the pupils a great big list of numbers to translate from the decimal to Roman numeral system. Hardly awe inspiring, is it? You have spent the time explaining what Roman numerals are, yet you are turning your back on a ready-made, A-grade context for generating enthusiasm. Instead, why not cast your class as their own century[10] within the Roman army with you, the teacher, as centurion? The pupils are told that they have been placed in charge of creating a new settlement in an area previously overrun with savages. Each child has to solve a variety of problems using Roman numerals based on their role within the century. Try out these roles for size:

- *Optio*. Your second-in-command. They have responsibility for checking the work of others. If there are any mistakes in the work brought to you, they will be answerable.

- *Aquilifer*. The standard-bearer of the legion and an incredibly important position. This legionnaire/pupil must ensure that the numerals written on the standard are correct. (This is a position of significant responsibility, but one that can be differentiated for pupils who are less secure in their understanding.)

---

10 A Roman *centuria* consisted of 100 men.

- *Signifer*. Another standard-bearer, this time for the signum of the century itself. They often acted as the banker for the legionnaires in the century. They must ensure that they pay the other legionnaires the correct amount of money.

- *Immunes*. Specialist soldiers who are immune from manual labour and guard duty. They could be specialists in whatever your imagination will stretch to and could have a range of special responsibilities.

- *Legionnaires*. Your bog standard troop. You could give them any number of duties to carry out, and one legionnaire could have a completely different set of tasks to carry out than another. How about translating the measurements for a new fort? Or scribing the number of slaves captured as prisoners of war in the most recent battle?

Differentiation by role within the Roman army. It's a tad eccentric, but it flies!

Binary is as easy as 1, 10, 11

"Do you speak robot?" It's a question that your pupils may not have been asked before, but it leads to their ears pricking up and the cogs of engagement starting to whir. Follow it up with, "How do you think robots and computers speak to each other?" and you are likely to get some awful vocoder impressions resembling a karaoke version of a Daft Punk song minus the backing track. "How do computers communicate?" is a valid question, though, and there is bound to be at least one smart cookie who knows it has something to do with code. If you offer children the chance to learn to speak robot, they will almost certainly jump at the chance. It's not as difficult as one might imagine either.

The basis for this language is the binary (or base 2) number system. In this system, there are only two digits: 0 and 1. So we start at 0, then 1, then ...? As we encounter the first bump in the road of learning how to speak robot, we use this as an opportunity for children to list all the possibilities for how we could show 2 in a number system that only has the digits 0 and 1. You might think there are only a few possibilities (i.e. 00, 01, 10, 11), but what about this one?

The correct answer is indeed 10, but I think I prefer Sarah's answer. Just when you think you've got the measure of them, they go and do something you didn't see coming.

The binary number system counts from 0 to 10 as follows:

Decimal	Binary
0	0
1	1
2	10
3	11
4	100
5	101
6	110
7	111
8	1000
9	1001
10	1010

Binary looks like it operates in an entirely different way to the decimal number system, but it does have one key feature that operates in exactly the same way:

	Binary	
	0	Start at 0
•	1	Then 1
••	10	Start back at 0 again, but add 1 on the left
•••	11	
••••	100	Start back at 0 again, and add one to the number on the left... ... but that number is already at 1 so it also goes back to 0 ... ... and 1 is added to the next position on the left
•••••	101	
•••••••	110	
••••••••	111	Start back at 0 again (for all 3 digits), add 1 on the left
•••••••••	1000	Start back at 0 again (for all 3 digits), add 1 on the left
••••••••••	1001	And so on!

Source: http://www.mathsisfun.com/binary-number-system.html

Once the pupils understand how binary works, I ask them, "What do you think robots talk to each other about?" Set the pupils a challenge to create a conversation between two robots where the answer to each question has to be about numbers and, furthermore, has to be given in binary form.

Robot 1: I am feeling rubbish today. The mechanic says that I need a new reverse quadrangle distribulifier. It's criminal how much they go for these days though!

Robot 2: I know, how much is it gonna set you back?

Robot 1: 11001 quid!

Robot 2: Daylight robbery!

Once the pupils have had time to plan out their conversations, you could ask them to perform their robot conversations in front of the rest of the class. The spectators could write down all of the binary numbers given and then try to translate them into decimal form.

A few points worth noting if you plan to do this activity:

- Ask the pupils to stick to numbers worth 25 or below (in decimal) as it can become rather difficult to make conversions between decimal and binary.[11]

- When writing numbers in binary, we can write a little 2 in subscript to the right of the number to show that it is a binary number and not a decimal number (e.g. 1011_2).

- Remember what I said about the importance of pronouncing numbers correctly: 451 is four-hundred-and-fifty-one not four-five-one? Well, the opposite is true of binary numbers: 1011 would be pronounced one-zero-one-one.

---

11 If you wish to make more complicated binary–decimal conversions, there is a nifty conver-tor at: http://www.mathsisfun.com/binary-decimal-hexadecimal-converter.html.

- If pupils act out their conversations then robot voices are mandatory. No half measures.

I hope this gives you an idea of what binary numbers are all about and how they can be used to great effect in the primary classroom. If you are still unsure, then just remember the old joke: "There are 10 kinds of people in this world, those who understand binary and those who do not."

There are further base number systems that you may wish to have a little look at, such as the hexadecimal system (base 16) which is also used in computing, and the sexagesimal system (base 60) which was invented by the ancient Sumerians. Both of these have significant applications in everyday life from the shade of colour in everything you see on a computer screen (often coded using hexadecimal) to the number of seconds in a minute and minutes in an hour (sexagesimal).

MATHEMAGICAL SURPRISE

One of the most refreshing things about working with primary aged children is their ability to find magic in anything. I think that we teachers should do everything in our power to make the world stay magical. Yet, by ensuring that our pupils acquire knowledge about what, how and why things happen, in many ways we take some of that magic away and replace it with facts. Facts are incredibly important, but so is magic. For this reason, it's great practice to sneak snippets of magic into our daily interactions with kids. Now, before you rush out buy a top hat and white rabbit, let's take a look at what is magic is through the eyes of a child:

- Magic is about tricking people.

- Magic only exists sometimes.

- Magic is Norwich City scoring.

- Magic is what Harry Potter does.

- Magic is being able to play the piano with your toes.

- Magic is knowing how to make people smile.

- Magic is what pandas are.

- Magic is the feeling you get when you find out something new.

- Magic is making your homework disappear.

Magic doesn't necessarily have to involve a wand, but it does need to include two key principles:

1   The task should be difficult or seem difficult initially.

2   It should be something that you could impress your gran with.

In terms of the primary maths curriculum, we must ensure that pupils continually gasp at the wonder in not knowing – at least to begin with. When I was a little boy, I thought that my dad was magic, but he never pulled a rabbit out of a hat or a coin from behind my ear. It was down to two things: he was great with numbers and he could make balloon animals. His skill with numbers included simple memory tricks where he would remember the phone number, postcode and number plate of seemingly anyone he had ever met, to mental arithmetic that seemed unnaturally quick for a human. His ability to solve any arithmetical question that I threw at him with speed and accuracy seemed miraculous to me. Nowadays, when all the information, games and videos of amusing cats you could ever want are only a click away, it is perhaps more difficult to wow children with such simple abilities. Except it isn't. Our reliance on technology for information and entertainment has actually resulted in many children being blown away by the power of the mind rather than of the computer, and our own knowledge rather than Wikipedia.

One of the most talented students I ever had was a bit of a human calculator who rarely experienced anything in the way of mathematical challenge in the confines of the primary classroom. The extension work teachers set for him seemed to be built on the premise of giving him more of the same rather than anything with any real challenge. In my first lesson with him, I challenged him to find out the sum of all of the digits from 1 to 100 in under five minutes. He set off at a frantic pace, pencil scratching at the paper as he blitzed through the first 20 digits. However, soon enough, the five minute time limit was up and he hadn't finished. Not even close. I told him that there was once a boy his age who had managed to do it in a matter of seconds. He didn't believe me: "How could he do that? Did he have a calculator? Did his teacher tell him the answer? Did he go on Google? What's the answer, anyway?"

The famous pupil in question was one of the greatest mathematicians of all time, Carl Friedrich Gauss. There are many stories about Gauss as a child prodigy, but in one he was supposedly set the task described above as punishment for not underlining the date and title (or something equally terrible). He astounded his teacher by not only coming up with the correct answer, but also by managing to do so almost instantaneously. There has been more than one suggestion for how Gauss managed to do this with such ease, including using triangular numbers. The one I like is that he quickly realised he could make pairs of numbers that equalled 101 by taking a number from either end of the number range, so 1 + 100 = 101, 2 + 99 = 101, 3 + 98 = 101, 4 + 97 = 101 and so on. There are 50 pairs to be made from the numbers 1 to 100, and so 50 lots of 101 equal 5050. Simple.

When I told my pupil that that I could show him how to work it out in under a minute with a simple trick, he didn't believe me and thought that it was impossible. The look on his face when the penny dropped was priceless, and he couldn't wait to go and show his mates his new technique.

If you are looking for a good trick to teach your class, then a nice place to start is a 'mind reading' trick. These work on the basis of asking people to think of a number and then to manipulate that number using a series of operations before revealing to them what their start number was. How about trying this one from the NRICH website:

1   Think of a number.

2   Double it.

3   Add 10.

4   Halve it.

5   Take away your original number.

6   Is your answer 5?[12]

You could get pupils to write their own mind reading tricks using this format. Another trick I like, which is also on the NRICH website, allows you to find out how old someone is while simultaneously working out their shoe size:

1   Write down your age.

2   Multiply it by $1/5$ of 100.

3   Add on today's date (e.g. 2 if it's the 2nd of the month).

4   Multiply by 20% of 25.

---

12   See http://nrich.maths.org/1051.

5   Now add on your shoe size (if it is a half size round to a whole number).

6   Finally, subtract 5 times today's date.

7   Show me your final answer.[13]

When you look at the answer, the digits in the thousands and hundreds are the age and the tens and ones digits are the shoe size: if the answer is 1105, the age would be 11 and the shoe size would be 5. You can see from this example that the delivery of the trick can be made either more or less difficult by using percentages and fractions (e.g. "Multiply it by $\frac{1}{5}$ of 100" could be simplified to "Multiply it by 20").

One trick that is a step beyond your standard times tables – the 142857 times table – produces an awesome pattern. Using a calculator, complete the following:

142857 x 1 =

142857 x 2 =

142857 x 3 =

142857 x 4 =

142857 x 5 =

142857 x 6 =

---

13 See http://nrich.maths.org/1051.

Can you see the cycle? Amazing! Try completing the times table up to 10. Does the pattern continue? Are there any multiples that yield unexpected results? Can you predict what 142857 x 14 will equal?

There are bucket loads of examples on the internet, but if you are looking for superb book with lots of number tricks then *Classroom Gems: Games, Ideas and Activities for Primary Mathematics* by John Dabell is a great resource.

A SLICE OF PASCAL'S TRIANGLE

I love triangles and I'm not afraid to show it:

I ask the kids to list as many reasons as they can think of as to why I might love triangles. Some previous suggestions have included:

- They look like spaceships.

- They have fewer sides to count than an octagon.

- They only have three sides and three is the magic number.

- They sometimes fit together to create nice patterns.

- They look like they would make something faster.

- Cake is always sliced into triangles and you love cake.

I tell the kids that although I'm a huge fan of triangles, I'm not the world's biggest enthusiast. I then flip up pictures of Pythagoras and Pascal on the board, and tell the pupils their names, explaining that they had such brilliant reasons for their own love of triangles that they went on to become incredibly famous mathematicians. We focus in on Blaise Pascal and look at a brief potted history of his life and achievements. You might be thinking, "Why would kids care about some dusty mathematician of yesteryear?" Well, we teach primary age pupils about famous writers and scientists, but mathematicians are rarely ever given a look-in. Children should learn that, although maths is at the core of almost everything we do, we would not be able to do half the things we can do without the people who worked hard to explore the vast possibilities of mathematics.

I then ask the children to make as many different triangles as they can by placing up to 15 round sweets in a variety of triangle patterns. They tend to try out a few different ways of placing the sweets before settling on laying them out as an equilateral triangle, like this:

We explore why they have chosen to place the sweets in this way and then recap on the name and properties of this particular triangle. I then show them this picture:

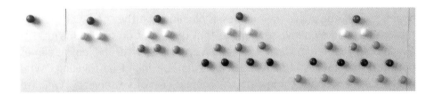

I ask them to jot down everything they can tell me about the picture on a sticky note. There is every chance here that you could be greeted with a vast range of responses, all of which will be useful and valid. Hopefully, the children will spot that there is a number pattern that ascends from three sweets in the first triangle to 15 sweets in the fourth triangle. Ask the children to work out how many sweeties will be needed for the next three triangles.

When they have figured this out, prepare to blow their minds! Ask the pupils to work out the number of sweets that would be needed for the hundredth triangle in the sequence. This request is usually met with a combination of furrowed brows, scratched heads, distractedly sharpened pencils and at least one child who looks as if they have just been asked to make a scale model of St Paul's Cathedral out of belly button fluff. Put the lid on and give them a few minutes to stew ...

Tell the class that you can work out the number of sweets required for any of the first 100 triangles in the sequence, and that they will be able to do this as well by the end of next lesson. All they need to do is ask for Mr Pascal's help (and make sure you've got plenty of sweets).

You will need some space for the next bit. Give each child a mini whiteboard and pen. Tell them that they are going to make a human triangle by sitting on the floor in a triangular formation. However, they are not going to make any old triangle. Oh no, they are going to make a human version of Pascal's triangle. Get them sitting down in a triangle, and ask the pupil at the top of the triangle to write the number 1 on their mini whiteboard. Inform the class that the number they need to write on their boards will be the sum of the boards of the two pupils sat above them on either side. Work through the triangle as a whole class. One of the first questions you'll get will be from the children sitting on the edges of the triangle: "What do I do – I only have a person above me on one side?" The answer is simple: if you only have one person above you then you have one plus nothing. They will soon realise that everyone sitting at the edges will equal 1. But will this always be the case? Then ask the pupils to wipe their mini whiteboards clean. Ask them all to stand up and tell them that they are going to make the triangle again, but this time they must sit in a different position. Tell them they are up against the clock, and that last year's class did it in a ridiculously quick time.

Off they go! Once they have completed the task, record the time and take a picture of the pupils in their completed Pascal's triangle. This serves three purposes:

1   It provides a brilliant starting point for the next lesson.

2   You can display it in your classroom and ask the kids to beat their time as a quick activity whenever motivation levels begin to drop.

3   It proves to the sheriff that you have not been messing about all lesson, but have, in fact, been studying one of the most interesting number patterns and encouraging pupils to work effectively as a team.

During the next lesson we use the picture of the completed human Pascal's triangle to study the range of patterns that exist inside it. Here are some simple ones to focus on:

• Symmetry. The triangle is symmetrical in its values throughout.

```
                               1
                            1     1
                         1    2    1
                      1    3    3    1
                   1    4    6    4    1
                1    5   10   10    5    1
             1    6   15   20   15    6    1
          1    7   21   35   35   21    7    1
       1    8   28   56   70   56   28    8    1
    1    9   36   84  126  126   84   36    9    1
  1   10   45  120  210  252  210  120   45   10    1
 1   11   55  165  330  462  462  330  165   55   11    1
1   12   66  220  495  792  924  792  495  220   66   12    1
1   13   78  286  715 1287 1716 1716 1287  715  286   78   13    1
1   14   91  364 1001 2002 3003 3432 3003 2002 1001  364   91   14    1
```

- Second diagonal. This follows the order in which we count upwards: 1, 2, 3, 4, 5, 6, 7, 8, 9, 10, 11, 12.

```
                                    1
                                 1     1
                              1     2     1
                           1     3     3     1
                        1     4     6     4     1
                     1     5    10    10     5     1
                  1     6    15    20    15     6     1
               1     7    21    35    35    21     7     1
            1     8    28    56    70    56    28     8     1
         1     9    36    84   126   126    84    36     9     1
      1    10    45   120   210   252   210   120    45    10     1
   1    11    55   165   330   462   462   330   165    55    11     1
1    12    66   220   495   792   924   792   495   220    66    12     1
1    13    78   286   715  1287  1716  1716  1287   715   286    78    13     1
1    14    91   364  1001  2002  3003  3432  3003  2002  1001   364    91    14     1
```

- Horizontal lines. If you add up all of the digits on a horizontal line, then you get this pattern as you move towards the base of the triangle: 1, 2, 4, 8, 16, 32, 64, 128, etc. (i.e. the numbers double each time).

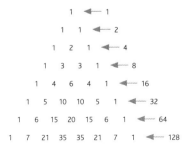

- Third diagonal. If you follow the line of the third diagonal you get, 1, 3, 6, 10, 15, 21, 28, etc. Hold on, didn't we see these numbers earlier when we were looking at making triangles out of sweets? It *is* the same pattern. They are triangular numbers.

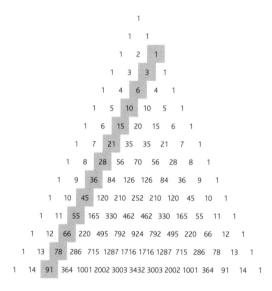

There are some more complex patterns that can also be found in Pascal's triangle, such as:

- Square numbers. The sum of the number next to it and the number that is below both of those numbers.

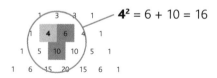

$4^2 = 6 + 10 = 16$

- The numbers that appear in the Fibonacci sequence.

So, next time someone asks what your favourite shape is, I hope that you give consideration to the humble triangle. It's what Pascal would have wanted.

So, there you have it, a whole chapter on numbers. If you have managed to get to this point, then hopefully I've succeeded in showing you that numbers are nothing to be afraid of but, in fact, can be something for children to marvel at!

Chapter 2
THE FOUR OPERATIONS

"Manners are not taught in lessons," said Alice. "Lessons teach you to do sums, and things of that sort."

"And you do Addition?" the White Queen asked. "What's one and one and one and one and one and one and one and one and one and one?"

"I don't know," said Alice. "I lost count."

"She can't do Addition," the Red Queen interrupted. "Can you do Subtraction? Take nine from eight."

"Nine from eight I can't, you know," Alice replied very readily: "but …"

"She can't do Subtraction," said the White Queen. "Can you do Division? Divide a loaf by a knife – what's the answer to that?"

"I suppose –" Alice was beginning, but the Red Queen answered for her. "Bread-and-butter, of course. Try another Subtraction sum. Take a bone from a dog: what remains?"

Alice considered. "The bone wouldn't remain, of course, if I took it – and the dog wouldn't remain; it would come to bite me – and I'm sure I shouldn't remain!"

"Then you think nothing would remain?" said the Red Queen.

"I think that's the answer."

"Wrong, as usual," said the Red Queen: "the dog's temper would remain."

"But I don't see how –"

Lewis Carroll, *Through the Looking-Glass* (1871)

I love this little section from *Through the Looking-Glass*, and think it sums up just how confused we can become when solving calculations involving the four operations. Addition, subtraction, multiplication and division are the crux of primary mathematics, and quite rightly occupy a substantial place in the primary curriculum. They are vital for the development of good numeracy skills and have wide ranging application in everyday life. However, in the wrong hands they can bore children to tears. Please don't turn your pupils into young arithmophobics.

Arithmophobia: we've all seen it and many of us have felt it ourselves. The minute the maths lesson starts the heads drop; beaming smiles turn to frowns and eyes drift upwards towards the clock, every second stretching out to what seems an eternity. The only thing worse than the monotony of repeating the same questions over and over again is the fear that at any moment you could be put on the spot. What if I don't know the answer? I never know the answer. I'm not some sort of human calculator! The really concerning thing with arithmophobia is that it is entirely contagious and, if left unchecked, your whole class can come down with it. You could even find yourself succumbing to arithmo-jitters yourself, draining your confidence in how you teach the subject. Thankfully, it is easily treated, requiring nothing more than a little understanding and a healthy dose of creativity. By the end of this chapter, you should be buzzing with plenty of ideas to turn your little ones not just into human calculators but into arithmetical acrobats.

ADDITION

Addition is the easiest of the four operations to grasp, as it is the operation that most naturally relates to straightforward counting upwards. In the early stages of learning addition, children will often use counting up on their fingers as the 'go to' strategy for adding. When working out 3 + 2, children will usually start with three fingers up and then put two more fingers up before counting them to make five. This makes complete sense: we tend to use our hands and fingers to demonstrate many things, such as giving directions, pointing out something of interest or indicating a preference.

However, this fine strategy starts to become slightly more cumbersome as the maths becomes more complex. It should be just another tool in our pupils' toolkits, not something that governs how they work. As the venerable Mickey Mouse is reputed to have said: "Arithmetic is being able to count up to twenty without taking your shoes off." The last thing you want is a classroom full of children with their shoes and socks off! What happens if they need to count to 21? What about the stench of post-PE cheesy feet? Children need to develop a mental agility around solving any question involving any one of the four operations, and the start of this process is learning simple number facts. Children need to work on their number facts, such as bonds to ten, from the earliest possible age and be able to recall them with both pace and accuracy.

PELMANISM

One way to work on developing pupils' understanding of number bonds is to play Pelmanism (otherwise known as concentration or pairs). This can be done by taking 11 small cards and writing on them the numbers from 0 to 10. Once you have made your cards, give them a shuffle and lay them face down on a table top. The pupil then has to turn over two cards at a time with the aim of making a number bond that equals ten (e.g. 0 + 10, 1 + 9, 2 + 8). If the pupil picks a correct pair, they leave the cards turned face up and pick again; if they are wrong, they turn them back over and the next pupil gets a go. This is great played in small groups or head to head. Alternatively, try placing a number of small items (e.g. counters, paper clips, Lego bricks, Multi-Link cubes) under plastic cups, so that you have 11 upside down cups covering objects of ascending value from 0 to 10. (You can write the value of the contents on the inside of the cup base for additional support, if necessary.) This has the further benefit of providing concrete examples of what each number actually represents.

One of the reasons that Pelmanism is so useful is that it provides the perfect 'in' for discussing one of the key properties of addition: commutativity. Commutativity means that you can reverse the terms in a sum, left to right, and it will still give you the same answer. For example:

a + b = b + a

1 + 2 = 2 + 1

The commutative property of addition is important because, once children grasp the fact that they can change the order of their sum and still get the same answer, they are free to work out the sum in the way that is most effective for them. For instance, 3 + 11 is more easily solved mentally if viewed as 11 + 3 (i.e. when we start with the largest number). By understanding this property, pupils are able to answer sums with greater confidence, pace and accuracy. It also provides an excellent contrast when covering subtraction, as this is the inverse of addition and is *not* commutative: meaning that correct order in subtraction is vital.

It all seems pretty simple so far, so where does it go wrong? One of the first common difficulties to occur is that of bridging through ten. This is where the sum of two numbers goes over the next ten: 9 + 5 = 14 or 16 + 7 = 23.

In both these examples, the sum of the two digits in the ones column goes above ten. Providing pupils have a solid understanding of place value (never assume this), they should know by now that the highest digit you can have in any column or place is 9. Therefore, when the sum of two digits in the ones column goes above ten, we must carry across a ten into the tens column.

Remember: without understanding the rules of the number system, we cannot work with numbers!

If your pupils have not grasped the idea of basic place value, then repeat until they are concrete in their understanding. Even with a solid comprehension of how place value works, children may still make arithmetical mistakes when adding together two numbers that bridge through ten. This is often because they try to jump straight to the answer. In which case, the solution here is to sloooowwwwwwwww dooooooooowwwwwn! If your pupils have a tendency to speed through work making careless errors ask them to check their work, check again and ask a friend.

Once pupils have the understanding that they can use their knowledge of basic number facts (such as bonds to ten), they will be more successful. Children need to see each set of ten as a numerical milestone. The way I approach this is to talk to the children about journeys. I tell them about trips I've been on, where I've had to make more than one stop on my route. At each stop we calculate how far I have travelled; first, adding to the next ten and then adding on the remaining distance for that leg.

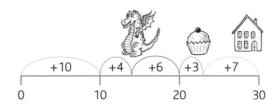

This number shows a journey where, initially, I had to drive 14 miles to drop off my pet dragon, Derrick, at the Dragon Day Care; followed by another nine miles to the bakery to pick up some cake for the teachers; then another seven miles to arrive at work. Once the pupils have grasped the idea, they can create little journeys of their own, mapping out a linear route using small plastic sports cones that are equally spaced apart, with different colour cones to signify tens.

Splitting the numbers into their separate parts is another successful strategy, providing that pupils have a solid understanding of the number system. Pupils must know that the 7 in 79 stands for seven tens and that the 9 stands for nine ones. Once the numbers have been split into tens and ones (possibly hundreds but unlikely at this stage) they can be added together as follows:

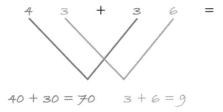

Once we are at this stage, we then recombine the numbers by adding the two totals together:

$$70 + 9 = 79$$

It is worth reminding pupils, once again, that the reason this works is because of the commutative property of addition: any sum can be calculated in any order.

Another trick worth mentioning is that of adding 'near multiples'. This is where you round one of the ones to ten and then readjust by subtracting or adding the amount you rounded up by at the end:

42 + 19 becomes 42 + 20 – 1

This is a really useful trick, but the term can be a little confusing because it uses the word 'multiple'. Children need to have this method clearly explained to them, preferably with the use of a hundred square and a number line. Ensure that the pupils can explain why you might use this method and what potential errors they could make (such as forgetting to subtract the amount rounded up by at the end).

Once children have achieved a good understanding of the basics of mental methods for addition, written methods can then be introduced. This should be done carefully using a step-by-step approach to every detail. Checking of understanding must be done at every stage, because this is when misconceptions can become apparent as there are a greater number of factors in play. With mental methods, we were just relying on the ability to manipulate numbers internally with the only external output being the answer. Once we progress on to written methods, we are asking pupils to show us, on paper, exactly what is going on inside their heads. I have seen bright, switched on youngsters completely lose their spark as soon as they are required to write down their workings because they are unsure of how exactly to set out their work. As teachers, we often neglect this part of the process because putting a digit in a box is not the difficult bit, is it? Well, actually, it can be really bloody hard for some children, especially if you want the digit in the correct box.

In my experience, the formal written method set out below is the most effective, so I generally teach this compact method in the first instance:

	H	T	O
	4	3	2
+	1	4	5
	5	7	7

Take your time and explain things thoroughly. I like to get pupils to jot down a step-by-step guide to how to set out their work, like this:

Step 1:

Set out your working:

	H	T	O
	4	3	2
+	1	4	5

Step 2:

Add your 'ones' column:

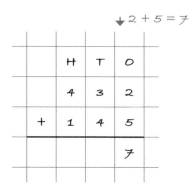

Step 3:

Add your 'tens':

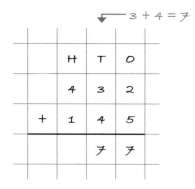

Step 4:

Add your 'hundreds':

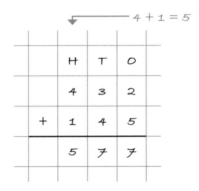

$$4 + 1 = 5$$

	H	T	O
	4	3	2
+	1	4	5
	5	7	7

An expanded method of this calculation is often taught prior to introducing the compact method. In the expanded method, the pupils use splitting again to separate the tens and ones. This results in the following:

	H	T	O	
	4	3	2	
+	1	4	5	
			7	$(2 + 5 = 7)$
		7	0	$(30 + 40 = 70)$
+	5	0	0	$(400 + 100 = 500)$
	5	7	7	

I am not a huge fan of the expanded approach for several reasons:

- It requires pupils to start adding from left to right (or tens to ones). This can be thoroughly confusing because, as soon as they are taught the compact method, they will be required to work from right to left (or from ones to tens).

- It is not actually any different from mental splitting, and is therefore not a progression in the pupils' understanding of how addition works. It is simply the writing down of a mental method.

- It increases the amount of working that needs to be written down, as well as the number of steps, therefore increasing the chance of a written error in the pupils' workings out.

However, some pupils do find this a useful strategy and, if it works for a particular child you are working with, I wouldn't discourage its use for them.

A relatively straightforward way to make boring column addition more fun is to supersize it by breaking out the mini whiteboards. Depending on how complex you wish to make the sums, give a pair or small group of pupils enough mini whiteboards to write one digit on each whiteboard, plus an extra one for the addition sign. You can either specify the digits the pupils must use, let them explore for themselves or, my own personal favourite, give the pupils the answers and ask them to write the questions. Children are used to answering the questions, not writing them, and very much relish the challenge of creating the questions themselves. This can be scaled up in difficulty by adding a caveat, such as, "You must include an example of carrying."

One potential area of frustration for the pupils is forgetting to add on the amount that has been carried over or regrouped into the next column:

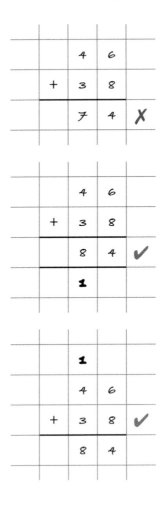

Remembering to add on what you have just carried under is not a difficult skill. But it isn't particularly exciting or enthralling either, so pupils hardly feel compelled to remember to do it. It is our job, therefore, to make it as enjoyable and interesting as possible so they don't forget. When I first started teaching, there were quite a few pupils in my class who struggled to remember to carry over, and the method that I came up with to demonstrate this concept was that of the 'yo-yo digit'. I start by showing the pupils how a yo-yo works, casting it down and watching it return back to my hand. I explain that, when adding using the column method, if the answer in any given column goes over 9, then a yo-yo number appears! It is cast down underneath the answer into the next column along. At this stage, I ask students whether yo-yos ever stay put? "No, they don't," comes the reply. "They fly back upwards!" I then explain that it is for this reason that the students must remember to add the value of the yo-yo digit to the total of that column (before the yo-yo disappears again). Pupils can even draw little yo-yo calculations themselves by putting the digit that is being regrouped or carried inside a picture of a yo-yo.

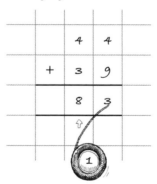

Another approach to explain this method was suggested to me by a colleague who had stumbled on a local news story about a cat that waited on the wall outside its house whenever its owners were out. Using the details of the story, my colleague would draw a little brick wall underneath the addition sums and, whenever there was something to carry over, she would draw a cartoon cat with the value carried over written on its chest. She said that the cat was so important to the owners that they would never forget it and would pick it up whenever they returned home.

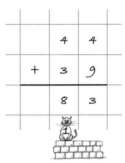

For those who prefer to regroup above the calculation, I have in the past explained the regrouping by talking about fireworks, human cannonballs or flying fish, as all these things fly up, but, sadly, and as we know, they always come back down again.

Another approach that works for numbers being written above or below the main body of the calculation is using the good old plane/train ticket upgrade approach. When you get above 9 in any given column (class) you have run out of room, and so number 1 is given an upgrade to a seat in the next class (column) up! The added bonus of this approach is that you can make a link to the fact that, as you progress from left to right through the columns, the place value of the digits (tickets) increases; more specifically, it increases by ten times the amount. This means that one ticket in the business class (tens) column is worth ten tickets in the economy class column, and a ticket in first class (hundreds) is worth 100 tickets in economy class.

SUBTRACTION

Subtraction is tough. For a start, at even its most basic level, it requires pupils to count backwards, which is far more difficult than counting forwards.

Before doing the even the simplest subtraction calculations with children, the most important thing to get nailed is the issue of commutativity (which we've covered above). As a reminder, commutativity is the ability to change the order of numbers in a calculation. Put simply, you can change the order of numbers in an addition calculation, but you can't with subtraction:

$3 + 7 = 10$ and $7 + 3 = 10$

However:

$10 - 3 = 7$ but $3 - 10 = -7$

If pupils aren't able to grasp this concept, they will be absolutely stumped when it comes to using formal written methods or when attempting to solve more complicated problems at a later stage. So, don't just tell them about it, get them to do it!

Give the pupils ten sweets (or counters, which are just as good, if nowhere near as tasty) and get them to explore the addition and subtraction calculations above. Try to resist the temptation of telling the pupils that the bigger number always goes on top, or first, as this is a lie and an unnecessary shortcut. Instead, explain that unlike addition calculations, which are actually pretty easy going and don't mind in which order they line up, subtraction calculations are a bit fussy and, as such, insist on being put in exactly the correct and appropriate order. Explain that most of the time this is done with the biggest number going first, but it isn't always the case. To reinforce this idea, ask the pupils to take a certain number of objects away which is a greater number than they currently possess – for example, take four pencils when they only have two, or take off three shoes when they are only wearing two, or put six pieces of scrap paper in the bin when they only have three. Repeat this regularly. Repeat this regularly. Repeat this regularly.

Once the pupils are getting used to this concept, introduce the idea of relating addition to subtraction. Explain how it is the inverse, or opposite, calculation and that this relationship can be super-useful when checking our work. Break out the number tabards at this point: these are mini whiteboard type things with a piece of string attached to the top two corners with sticky tape to create half a sandwich board. Group the children, ideally into fives. Each child gets a tabard and a board marker. I then write three numbers on the board that can be used to create addition and subtraction calculations:

12   8   20

I tend to set out place-markers using hoops or coloured card (or even chairs if you're feeling brave), to mark each part of the calculation. The aim is to see how quickly they can make all the possible addition and subtraction calculations using the three numbers on the board:

12 + 8 = 20

8 + 12 = 20

20 – 8 = 12

20 – 12 = 8

Each child takes the role of either one of the numbers or one of the symbols (though make sure that the same child is not putting themselves forward to be a symbol each time in the hope of an easy ride). Make sure that you take the time to address any mistakes and to point out the inverse relationship between addition and subtraction after each set of numbers. Explain how they can use this inverse relationship to check their work:

13 – 7 = 6

Therefore:

6 + 7 = 13

Also, pay particular attention to the fact that, although you can create two subtraction calculations out of the three numbers, the answers will be different. (With two different addition calculations with the same numbers the answers are the same, of course.) This method works because it is a damn sight more fun wearing a mini whiteboard and shuffling your group into the correct places than just writing the calculations out and holding it up in the vague hope that your hard work will be rewarded with a pleasing word from teacher.

Once the children are comfortable with subtracting numbers in the correct order, and are able to check their work with an inverse calculation, it is time to move on to more formal methods. As with addition, the 2014 national curriculum places a great deal of importance on the use of formal written methods. The curriculum asks for these to be introduced at a younger age, with pupils in Year 3 being required to carry out column subtraction involving decomposition (or breaking down numbers into their constituent elements). My advice would be to take a good long look at your pupils and gauge their readiness. Expose them to formal written methods too early and you risk devaluing the progress they have made developing mental methods of working; too late and you risk not ticking all of the national curriculum's many boxes. (I'll leave it to you to work out which one is more important and act accordingly.)

Once the lovelies are ready for written methods involving decomposition, I tell them the story of Robin Hood, introducing the moral idea of stealing from the rich to give to the poor. Robin Hood lends himself incredibly well to being the central character in my explanation of subtraction involving decomposition. We start with a calculation:

	5	2
−	1	7

In this example, 7 cannot be subtracted from 2 because we cannot take 7 away from 2 without going into negative numbers. This is a good opportunity to take a brief foray into explaining why we do not want to go into negative numbers by introducing the character of the Sheriff of Nottingham as the dastardly villain who would chop off your mother's fingers for falling behind with her tax payments! Robin Hood comes to our rescue here. Adorned in his customary green tights, Robin unleashes an arrow right through the heart of the rich, taking only what he needs to help the poor settle their debts, and thereby avoiding us from going into negative numbers:

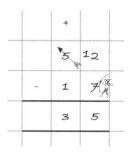

It is important to reiterate the fact that Robin is stealing not borrowing. Decomposition is often explained as borrowing – for example, with 1 being 'borrowed' from a next-door neighbour. I used to do this when I first trained as a teacher using a raft of awful accents to show how we could borrow 1 from whoever was next door (a bit like borrowing a cup of sugar). However, borrowing implies that you are going to return it at some point, and this is not the case with decomposition: it is flagrant and unapologetic theft.

Continuing this theme, another character you can call on to weave a little bit of storytelling into subtraction is Burglar Bill. Many children encounter this story in Key Stage 1 and will already be familiar with Bill. His catchphrase of, "I'm having that", provides a super prompt for reminding the pupils when to 'steal 1' from the next-door number digit that lives in the column to the left. When working through examples in groups or as a whole class, the cacophony of pupils chirping, "I'm having that", in their very best cockney accents, as they move 1 across is joyous to behold. (I like to draw Burglar Bill exiting the scene of the crime with his swag bag bulging with the numbers he has stolen.)

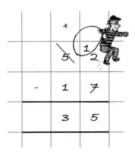

The Burglar Bill link also helps when confronted with a problem like this one:

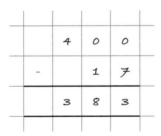

This idea of having to take 1, not only from the immediate neighbouring column but also from the next one along too, is notoriously difficult for children to grasp. However, explain that it is jolly hard work heaving a wide-screen TV or a three-piece-suite over not one but two neighbours' fences, so it's a good idea to have a rest after each fence before carrying the 1 over the final obstacle:

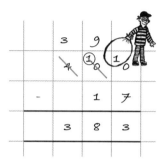

So, there you have it: subtraction. It's not as bad as everyone thinks and with a little effort can even become vaguely enjoyable(ish).

MULTIPLICATION

Multiplication relies on sound recall of multiplication facts, or times tables as they are commonly known. The general order for approaching the learning of tables is to start with multiples of 2 and 10 before moving on to multiples of 5, then multiples of 3 and 4. Pupils then progress on to learning multiples of 6, 7, 8 and, finally, 9. The 2014 national curriculum now states that pupils should learn up to the 12 times table by the age of 9, and there has been some significant grumbling over the feasibility of this. A common complaint from teachers is that they already have too much to cover and don't have the time to spend lessons drilling pupils in their times tables. However, times tables are a necessary, though not insignificant, pain. A firm grasp of times tables pays off in the long term, and is vital for providing a solid arithmetical foundation for future problem-solving.

When it comes to teaching times tables, a nice idea or principle is to SMASH them to pieces! The five principles behind SMASHing times tables are as follows:

1   Short and sweet

2   Mix it up!

3   Arrangement

4   Stir and stimulate

5   Hammer away

SHORT AND SWEET

Times tables are like cabbage or broccoli to children: they are hardly any child's preferred choice of diet, but they are full of the vital nourishment they need in order to function well. With this gustatory metaphor in mind, let's reconsider times tables and compare them to plain rice: filling but devoid of flavour. Rice can be delicious when accompanied by something exotic, but consumed on its own in large quantities, it is uninspiring at best. The message here is that a lesson where the sole focus is on the learning of times tables is a bland one.

However, rice goes well with so many things, and so do times tables. I try to incorporate a little times tables work into every single primary mathematics lesson. For the last couple of years, I've spent at least seven minutes of every lesson on them and on related mental arithmetic work. I've found this to be the optimal portion of times tables sustenance in order to provide the diner with enough to sate their hunger, while still having them wanting to come back for seconds. In some lessons, I will give the pupils more input while exploring particular times tables in greater detail, but never to a point where all they have covered in a lesson are times tables.

The best way I have found to incorporate daily times tables practice into every lesson has been through the use of multiplication grids (see the Appendix for some examples). These are relatively hassle free and fit well with the other principles of SMASH: they ensure that times tables are not presented in a linear fashion, they encourage pupils to embrace the commutative aspect of multiplication and they stir up a sense of competition, regardless of ability level, allowing pupils to hammer away at their tables work both at school and at home.

While on the notion of keeping it short and sweet, it is also important that the pupils aim for this in their answering of times tables questions. Mastery of times tables should not be judged solely on 'knowing' the multiplication facts, but also on the speed at which they can be recalled. If a pupil takes more than a few seconds to answer a times tables question, then they need further work on that times table.

MIX IT UP!

The most common mistake we make when teaching pupils times tables is to assume that a child has grasped a times table because they can repeat it parrot fashion in ascending order. Put simply, if a child has to start from 1 x each time they want to work out an answer, then they don't know that times table well enough. They need to be able to recall multiplication facts going forwards, backwards or out of order, so that they can solve related division calculations, and, most importantly, they need to be able to do all of this with pace. This can be a tall order for many children, but we are not doing them any favours by lowering our expectations. We should be aspiring to more than them simply counting upwards in multiples.

I've found it useful to look at pupils' progress in times tables through a graduated approach. Pupils who can recall multiples in ascending order would be classed as having an *emerging understanding*; if they can recall facts out of order then they can be considered to have a *firm understanding*; if they can use their multiplication facts quickly to solve related division calculations or 'fill in the missing digit' style calculations then I'd consider them to have an *advanced understanding*. Viewing the learning of times tables in this way gives greater importance to mastery of a key area of numeracy development. It also allows pupils to work on a particular times table to a certain level, and then move on to other times tables, revisiting the initial one at a later stage to extend their understanding to the next level.

Once again, the grid approach (see Appendix) is perfect for ensuring that pupils become used to working on times tables out of sequential order. As the level of difficulty increases, new times tables are introduced to the grid, but the previously learned times tables remain. This provides pupils with further drill in the areas they have worked on previously, sharpening their recall with every grid completed.

ARRANGEMENT

Taking a look at the way that the numbers are arranged within times tables gives pupils a deeper understanding of what times tables actually are and, crucially, how they interact with the number system. Furthermore, it becomes vital that we reinforce the fact that multiplication has a commutative property, and that swapping the digits around can dramatically reduce the difficulty of a given multiplication question. We sometimes take it for granted that children will recognise this aspect automatically, but they will often overlook this as a strategy for solving a multiplication calculation. Arrays can work wonders for explaining this concept:

1   Invite the pupils to work out a given multiplication calculation, such as 3 x 5, by placing dots (or counters, sweets, smiley faces, kittens, etc.) in three rows of five, like so:

2   Ask them to count up the total number of dots and write the total next to their dots.

3   Ask them to do the same for 5 x 3 alongside their previous working:

4   Discuss how three columns of five give us the same number of dots as five columns of three.

Repeat this process with several examples and it shouldn't be long before they have cracked it. By teaching this simple rule, you are dramatically reducing the number of multiplication facts that kids have to memorise. We've already explored the importance of looking for patterns in developing sound numerical understanding. Times tables are no different, so exploring the patterns that exist in them is time well spent.

For example, if we write out the 6 times table we get the following:

6 x 1 = 6
6 x 2 = 12
6 x 3 = 18
6 x 4 = 24
6 x 5 = 30
6 x 6 = 36
6 x 7 = 42
6 x 8 = 48
6 x 9 = 54
6 x 10 = 60
6 x 11 = 66
6 x 12 = 72

Can they spot the pattern?

How about now?

6 x 1 = 6
6 x **2** = 1**2**
6 x 3 = 18
6 x **4** = 2**4**
6 x 5 = 30
6 x **6** = 3**6**
6 x 7 = 42
6 x **8** = 4**8**
6 x 9 = 54
6 x **10** = 6**0**
6 x 11 = 66
6 x **12** = 7**2**

We can see that whenever we multiply an even number by 6 the digit in the ones column matches the number that we are multiplying by:

2 x 6 = 12

4 x 6 = 24

6 x 6 = 36

What about if we take a look at the 9 times table more closely?

1 x 9   = 09
2 x 9   = 18
3 x 9   = 27
4 x 9   = 36
5 x 9   = 45
6 x 9   = 54
7 x 9   = 63
8 x 9   = 72
9 x 9   = 81
10 x 9 = 90

The relationship between the tens and ones columns is the interesting bit, obviously. The ones column descends from 9 down to 0, while the tens column ascends from 0 to 9. Not only that, but if you add the digits together, then the answer will always be 9.

As well as spotting numerical patterns in times tables, visual patterns can be extremely useful too. I first stumbled across using visual patterns with times tables in the work of Tony Biesanz. He has some useful videos on YouTube explaining, among other ideas, how to use visual patterns to explore times tables. In one example he uses the four times table to draw a star.[1]

First, draw a circle and place points for 0 through to 9 around the circumference of the circle at equidistant intervals.

---

1   See https://www.youtube.com/watch?v=N1ALx5q6jO4. For more videos, check out his MisterNumbers channel at: https://www.youtube.com/channel/UCNab1XwWR1KnF53DUmTipEw.

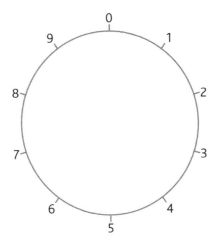

Then join the dots by going through the four times table in ascending order and drawing a line between the points based on the digit in the ones column, so 0 joins to 4, 4 joins to 8 and 8 then joins to 2 (because 2 is in the ones column for 12). If we continue to repeat the pattern, what we get is:

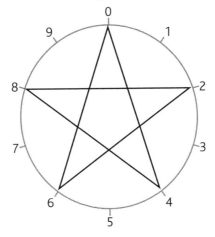

The really incredible thing about these patterns is that each times table, from 1 to 10, has a corresponding partner that will create the same pattern in reverse. The partners with corresponding patterns are the number bonds to 10: 1 and 9, 2 and 8, 3 and 7, 4 and 6, and 5.

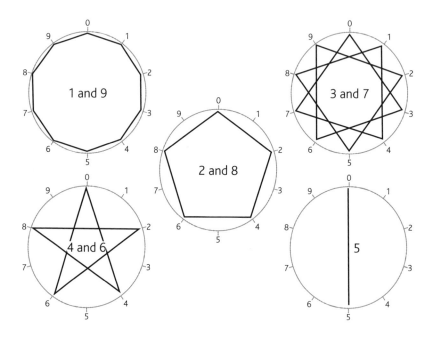

There is a fun property, which can be useful for checking your answer, that lurks within the 3 times table. If you take any multiple of 3, and add the digits from the multiple, they will always equal another multiple of three:

36: 3 + 6 = 9 or 3 x 3

33: 3 + 3 = 6 or 3 x 2

30: 3 + 0 = 3 or 3 x 1

27: 2 + 7 = 9 or 3 x 3

Or even:

2997: 2 + 9 + 9 + 7 = 27 or 3 x 9

Ask the children to use a calculator to multiply any number they like by 3 and see if the property remains true.

With all of these patterns, children gain a real sense of achievement as they unlock the beautiful world of numbers for themselves. Either that or they'll be chuffed that they have fewer times tables to memorise.

STIR AND STIMULATE

The real key to times tables success is supplementing the hard work and repetitive approach with activities from which the children will get a genuine buzz. Along with encouraging pupils to spot patterns, a sure fire way to stir some interest in the learning of times tables is to encourage some competition. There are tons of way to do this: from having a class league table or a points system to full blown approaches like Times Table Rock Stars.[2] Contrary to what some touchy-feely types might have you believe, children thrive when challenged and relish the opportunity to duel mathematically with their fellow peers. It just has to be dressed up in the appropriate clothing.

I am a passionate believer in the power of movement during mathematics lessons. A fantastic way of making times tables more exciting and relevant, especially for those who prefer to be on their feet than on their backsides, is to carry out some times tables circuit training every so often. This approach ensures that not only do pupils' brains hurt from challenging times table work, but they also get a chance to exercise the nine-tenths of their bodies below their necks too.

This method works best if you can do it in the playground or the school hall, but it can be adapted to work in a classroom. The idea is that you make several 'stations' where pupils have to use times tables to solve questions, but also that each station requires some form of physical activity. A simple example of this would a series of 'missing gap' times tables questions where pupils are required to pass a football as many times as their answer before moving on to the next question. The key is to make the stations simple to set up, simple to follow and simple to score, but with an appropriate level of challenge to stir a sense of competition. A great way to do this is to link in questions that involve division or square numbers that pupils must use

---

2   See https://ttrockstars.com/.

their multiplication facts to answer. Have a look at this sample circuit with a selection of stations:

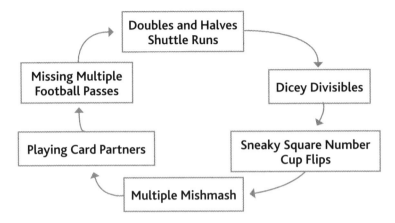

1   Missing Multiple Football Passes. Sticky notes with 'missing gap' multiplications on them are placed face down on the plastic sports cone in the middle. The first pupil runs to the cone, flips over the first sticky note and shouts it out to the rest of the group. Pupils work out the missing multiple, then complete as many passes with a football as the answer, before the next pupil runs to the central cone and repeats the process.

2   Doubles and Halves Shuttle Runs. Place a set of number cards on either of the two start cones. Pupils take it in turns to flip over a number card from alternating piles. When a card in the first pile is flipped over, the pupils have to double the number and run that many shuttle runs between their group. When they flip over a card from the second pile, they halve the number and run that many shuttle runs.

3   Dicey Divisibles. Prepare a set of sticky notes with two-digit products of times tables that the pupils know on each one. Once you have a decent set (30 should do) scrunch up each note individually into a ball and spread them out. The pupils take it in turns to roll a dice (large foam dice work best) and then find a sticky note with a number on it that is divisible by their dice number.

4   Sneaky Square Number Cup Flips. Prepare a set of cards with the square numbers to 12 x 12 on them. Shuffle the cards and place them face down on a table. Place 12 paper cups on the table. The first pupil flips a card over and works out what the square root of the number is (e.g. if the card says 81, the square root is 9). If the square root answer is even, then the pupils have to make sure that the same number of cups are flipped facing upwards; if the square root is an odd number, then they must flip the appropriate number of cups facing downwards.

5   Multiple Mishmash. Place sticky notes with a times table calculation on each of them on one wall (or the floor on one side of the room). Place the answers to the calculations on another set of notes of a different colour on the wall or floor on the opposite side of the room. Place an empty bin in between the sets of questions and answers. The pupils line up behind the bin and take it in turns to sprint out and collect a sticky note from the question side, before finding the corresponding answer on the other side. Once they have found a pair, they stick them together and dash back to chuck them in the bin. You can also ask the pupils to repeat this game in reverse, with them getting the answers first before heading to the questions.

6   Playing Card Partners. Prepare a set of sticky notes containing products from times tables up to 10 x 10 that the pupils know. Lay out a pack of playing cards with the face cards removed (face up for easy, face down for difficult). Pupils must pick a sticky note, then find a

pair of playing cards which, when multiplied together, will equal the number on the sticky note.

The circuit is just the start. These activities are so easily adapted and altered that the possibilities are endless. Imagine how brilliant a full-blown mathematical assault course could be? Or how about staging your very own Mathslympics? And why limit these ideas just to times tables? They could be used for drilling any type of four operations arithmetic. The only limitations are your imagination, available space and the school's health and safety policy.

For a simpler way of sprucing up your arithmetic drill, how about creating your very own question balloons? The procedure is simple enough:

Step 1: Blow up balloon.

Step 2: Scrawl relevant questions on said balloon in board marker pen.

Step 3: Go back to step 1 and start all over again, because it is better for the pupils do step 2 themselves. You may get a little out of breath here.

Step 4: Pupils throw question balloons to each other, answering whichever question is closest to their right thumb.

Step 5: Pupils cross out questions on the balloon with a board marker as they answer them.

Step 6: When they have answered all the questions, they can pop their balloon to signify that they have been victorious!

For an added level of difficulty, a 'killer question' can be inserted into the balloon on a small scrap of paper, which must be answered after the balloon has been popped.

Another cracking way to work with times tables (as well as any other form of arithmetic or number properties) is to play bingo. Instead of 'two little ducks' or 'jump and jive', think '2 x 11' or '7 x 5'. To make it more challenging, chuck in some addition or subtraction first to extend it to a two-step problem – for example, '7 plus 4 then multiply by 2' or '6 minus 9 multiplied by 5'.

Remember, mental agility is king.

HAMMER AWAY

Times tables are ideal conduits for teaching children the value of perseverance and resilience, as they are rarely mastered quickly. Put simply, times tables success does not happen overnight and pupils need to realise and be warned about this. It will take time and plenty of repetition for most pupils to become proficient in their application of times tables. They need to hammer away at them every day without fail. A sure fire way to speed up the acquisition of times tables is to involve parents as much as possible. It doesn't take a genius to figure out that the pupils who practise both at school and at home are more likely to pick up their times tables quickly.

A WORD ON TIMES TABLES 'PRODUCTS'

The market for times tables aids is ever increasing and, with the continual rise in mobile devices and apps, people have more choice than ever as to how they can support their little darlings with their learning at school and at home. The products on the market for teaching times tables are wide ranging and one could write a rather boring book just listing them. However, they vary greatly in quality. By all means explore the possibilities, but don't be fooled by gimmicks claiming to be the magic solution. Keep in mind the SMASH principle and you won't go far wrong.

WRITTEN METHODS

As with all the four operations, there is a move towards ensuring that pupils are accomplished in their use of written methods for multiplication. There is a plethora of written methods for multiplication. My preferred ones are the grid method (multiplication with partitioning) and the traditional long multiplication method of laying out. The grid method is a solid starting point for venturing into written methods because it builds on mental methods and minimises place-keeping errors due to being set out neatly in a grid. I use the method as follows:

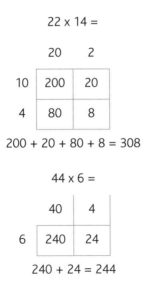

$$22 \times 14 =$$

	20	2
10	200	20
4	80	8

$$200 + 20 + 80 + 8 = 308$$

$$44 \times 6 =$$

	40	4
6	240	24

$$240 + 24 = 244$$

The traditional column method can pose greater difficulty for pupils due to the more intricate nature of knowing the correct order in which to multiply the digits. As explained earlier in this chapter, breaking down the individual steps is vital. The way I tend to approach this is to enlarge the calculation and then draw different coloured arrows that are numbered to show each step:

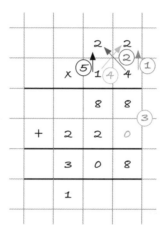

And that's all I've got to say about written methods of multiplication. Bit short? Maybe. There's a reason for that though. If every primary teacher taught multiplication in the same ratio as this section (about five times more work on mental methods and times tables compared to the time spent on teaching written methods) then pupils would be in a far better position to problem-solve when they hit secondary school. Times tables simply must be the focus – don't marginalise them too early.

DIVISION

Division is, without doubt, the least popular of the four operations. A straw poll on the areas of mathematics that most people associate with confusion and stomach churning dread almost always yields the same result: the dislike of division is as common as the belief that the gruff school dinner lady was not actually a lady at all.

Every time I teach division, I try to think up a new way to present it. As I mentioned previously, "Anyone can feed sweets to sharks", comes from a short piece of in-lesson drama that I use to explain division. The first lesson in the series begins with the teacher (me) entering the room dressed as a deep-sea fisherman (yellow waterproof mac optional but highly advised). I explain that I am a scientist working for the Society of Somalian Sugar Sharks (alliteration works best when trying to introduce an element of absurdity) and that my job is to care for a rare breed of shark: the only vegetarian shark in the world. The pupils are then told that this particular shark feeds only on sweets, and that because of this they need feeding twice a day by me and my team. At this point, I usually ask the pupils to spend a few minutes thinking in groups about what they will need to consider when feeding Somalian sugar sharks. Some of the answers you get here are brilliant, with the best one ever being, "To make sure that you are not dressed in bright colours, otherwise you might look like a sweetie yourself". Following this, I usually split the class into groups to work out how many sweets they would feed to each shark, given a particular number of sweeties and a particular number of sharks.

How many sweets would you give to each shark if you had 11 sweets and three sharks?

For this part, you can split the pupils up into sharks and scientists and get them to act it out, or you can use a small group to demonstrate to the rest of the class. Once the pupils have worked through several examples, I usually get them to feed back to the class what they have been doing, the process they went through and the answers they got.

For the next step in the sugar shark drama, you will need a small number of pupils who are not afraid to act as sharks (simple shark hats made out of laminated pictures of a shark head help the pupils to get into character). The teacher still plays the role of the scientist who feeds the sharks. The teacher picks a number of sweets that will not share equally between the sharks (pupils), such as 11 sweets for three sharks. The teacher demonstrates sharing the sweeties out to the sharks, who greedily chomp on them until the problem occurs of not having enough sweets to give each shark another one (the remainder).

At this point, I ask each of the sharks how they would feel if I gave the other shark another sweet, but didn't give one to them. I also ask the rest of the class to spend a minute or two discussing what I should do next. We play around with the idea until we get to the solution of not feeding the sharks any more unless they can all have one, because all division should be fair and equal. We talk about what we could call the amount of sweeties that are left over, before introducing the word 'remainder'. The pupils then work through some examples themselves. I have also asked the pupils to film their own sugar shark drama episode to demonstrate the idea of remainders, which is then shown to the rest of the class.

I have another tried and tested method for introducing the formal method of written short division. The formal method of written division is very different to the other four operations: it does not look anything like the other three, which tend to stand in a more orderly manner, in regimented columns. The thing that goes over the top of the number that you are dividing, you know the bit I mean, well, I've always thought it looks a bit like a bus stop. It is for this reason that one day, a couple of years ago, I found myself in the art room (not my natural environment) with a cardboard box and some red paint. My class had just been doing some work on forms of transport and how they travelled to school in their geography lessons. It transpired that several children in the class had more than a passing interest in London buses. So, with this in mind, I set about creating my first Division Bus. More budget *Art Attack* than *Pimp My Ride*, I slathered the box in red paint and crudely drew on the necessary appendages of wheels and headlights. Next, I attached two lengths of yellow string to form shoulder straps. There it was, a thing of beauty, my first Division Bus.

When I unveiled it in front of the class, there were 'oohs' and 'aaahs' from all corners of the room, mainly to do with the burning question of how I had managed to wedge myself inside such a small box! To use the Division Bus to its full potential you first need to set up your bus stop. I tend to project a background on the whiteboard with a division bracket as the bus shelter. I position a number of chairs under the shelter (division bracket) with a mini whiteboard and pen on the seat, and I pin up some bus timetables either side of the board to set the scene. Pick a number of children to be passengers waiting at the bus stop based on the number of chairs you have laid out. It helps if you have costumes for them to dress up in as every rough, tough boy secretly relishes the opportunity to dress up like a granny. Get the pupils to sit at the bus stop with a single digit written on their mini whiteboard. They must not show the rest of the class their number until the bus arrives in order to keep the suspense rolling. As the bus pulls up to the stop, the driver (pupil) shows the rest of the pupils a mini whiteboard with the divisor written on it. As soon as the divisor has been unveiled, the passengers at the bus stop spin around their mini whiteboards to show the dividends. At this point, every pupil in the class who is not either a driver or at the bus stop dashes to scrawl down the working out and answer to ensure that they might just get picked to be the next bus driver.

When the pupils have a solid understanding of how to use the short division method, the long division method can be introduced. This method enables pupils to divide by numbers that are larger than 12. If you have to teach it, you could do a whole lot worse that visiting this website, which shows a very good demonstration of long division: www.mathsisfun.com/numbers/long-divisionpanimation.html.

Despite there being lots of different modified and shortened ways of carrying out this type of calculation, the one demonstrated on the website above is the most common and the easiest to follow. The core idea to reinforce in this method is the 'bringing down' of digits from underneath the division bracket. When I was growing up, one of my favourite computer games was a cracking little number called *Lemmings*. The aim of the game was to navigate a certain percentage of your lemmings around a map while ensuring they didn't plunge off the edge of a cliff to their demise. This idea of lemmings diving is a great way to remind the pupils to bring down the necessary numbers from the division bracket.

A WORD ON CALCULATORS

By time you read this book, the thinking could have changed, but the 2014 national curriculum suggests that calculators should only be introduced towards the end of Key Stage 2, and only if pupils have achieved a solid understanding of the basics. The reasoning is that by introducing calculators at the start of Key Stage 2, pupils will become reliant on them for even basic arithmetic. I'm sure this would actually be the case if pupils were given calculators in every lesson and the teacher allowed the pupils to use them for every question. However, we are professionals and, with a bit of judgement, I am of the belief that calculators can be incredibly useful tools for pupils throughout Key Stage 2 and even in Key Stage 1.

A crucial area of development for any pupil is encouraging them to work with greater independence. In mathematics, one of the most important aspects of this is getting pupils into the habit of checking their own work for mistakes. This is one area where a calculator can come into its own. By providing pupils with calculators, and teaching them how to check their work effectively, they can obtain far more immediate feedback on their work than is possible if they rely solely on the teacher to check it. Of course, there are many other methods for checking work, and I am not suggesting that a calculator is necessarily the best approach for all circumstances, but it can be a very effective tool.

Another use for calculators is to deploy them in contexts where the calculation element of the lesson is playing second fiddle to a more powerful objective: developing investigative skills. In an investigation, we are often asking pupils to use skills they have already learned to tackle a far wider and more abstract problem. The key aim of such an activity is to get them thinking for themselves, and part of that is working out how they can work most efficiently. Using a calculator to trial and improve working and answers is a valuable learning opportunity for the older primary pupil – for example, asking pupils to find out the four consecutive numbers that add up to 268.

The main reason that calculators can be effective in the primary age phase is simply that they can be great fun. Anything that encourages children to play around with numbers and calculations shouldn't be sniffed at. Here are a few fun ideas to get you started:

- **Beat the calculator**. One person has a calculator, the other has only their brain and they race to answer questions.

- **Messing about writing words**. Try 1 – 0.2266 or 30218017 x 2 before turning the calculator upside down to reveal a word.

- **Closest wins**. Pupils have ten seconds to estimate the answer to a difficult calculation; closest answer wins.

For some superb ideas about what can be done with a calculator have a look at the NRICH website,[3] which illustrates brilliantly just what can be achieved with a calculator when wielded well in the right hands.

---

3   See http://nrich.maths.org/public/leg.php?group_id=37&code=5028#results.

IN CONCLUSION

Over the years, I've come up with countless different ways of explaining the four operations and, to be honest, I wouldn't be able to tell you which one I think works the best. Different classes like different approaches. The unifying factor is that it feels a damn sight more interesting learning about yo-yos, fireworks, human cannonballs, burglars, Robin Hood, Somalian sugar sharks, buses and lemmings than dredging through some dull textbook, worksheet or PowerPoint that has nothing to excite other than a flashy colour scheme. Not to mention the fact that you can take these ideas as a starting point and present them in all manner of ways through storytelling, drama, artwork and so on.

Making maths memorable by being, erm, zany and far from what the pupils expect has massive benefits. First, when it comes to covering operations such as division again, I can refer to the sugar sharks and the children usually remember the process and approach we went through. I cannot say the same of baldly enquiring, "Remember when we did column multiplication ..." I've spoken to children several years later who tell me that they still think about sharks when solving division problems, or greedy crocodiles when looking at equations that contain inequalities. Second, it serves to reinforce the message that maths can be fun and that it is not simply a subject based on textbooks and the answering of questions which are either right or wrong. Children form early positive memories associated with maths, so if you do it with imagination and verve it becomes less of a Marmite subject. Or it remains a Marmite subject, but a version of Marmite that everyone likes.

Chapter 3
GEOMETRY

Once upon a time there was a sensible straight line who was hope-lessly in love with a dot. "You're the beginning and the end, the hub, the core and the quintessence," he told her tenderly, but the frivolous dot wasn't a bit interested, for she only had eyes for a wild and unkempt squiggle who never seemed to have anything on his mind at all. All of the line's romantic dreams were in vain, until he discovered … angles! Now, with newfound self-expression, he can be anything he wants to be – a square, a triangle, a parallelogram. … And that's just the beginning!

Juster Norton, *The Dot and the Line:
A Romance in Lower Mathematics* (1963)

Geometry is an ace area of mathematics and one that children, almost universally, seem to enjoy. Of all of the topics that we get to delve into when teaching primary maths, geometry is the one that manifests itself most beautifully, and most obviously, in the world around us. My guess is that, if you have managed to get this far through the book, you too have begun to see that maths can indeed be beautiful – in which case you'll love this chapter. If you have just picked up this book to have a flick through and stumbled on this page, keep reading – you will love this chapter.

Unlike numbers, which require an understanding of how to handle them to truly appreciate their attributes, shapes and movement are far easier to digest. As I write this on a superbly sunny Saturday afternoon in the Millennium Library, in Norwich, I am lucky enough to be witnessing an incredible celebration of shape and space coming together just outside the window.

When I arrived a few hours ago, there were a selection of cardboard boxes of various sizes stacked in a seemingly random order by the front door. What I can see out of the window as I now type is 'The People's Tower' – a replica of the St Peter Mancroft church tower – which was designed by Oliver Grossetête to mark the opening of the annual Norfolk and Norwich Festival, made entirely out of cardboard boxes and packaging tape. People all of ages are stacking, sliding and taping boxes together as they build one of the most incredible things I've ever seen constructed entirely from cardboard![1]

I didn't expect this when I went to the library this morning, and I am in awe of it. The crowds heave this magnificent masterpiece upwards to slide

---

1 See http://news.bbcimg.co.uk/media/images/74768000/jpg/_74768683_74764877.jpg

another layer underneath, and I am reduced to simply gawping in wonder. I am left with questions: how tall is it? How many boxes have they used? How far would all of the packaging tape stretch if laid end to end? But one question rings out above all: how can we recreate the sense of admiration and wonder I am currently experiencing through our teaching of geometry at primary school?

Now, before you venture to your nearest supermarket to nick as many cardboard boxes as you can lay your mitts on, pause please. I am not suggesting that we all go and build a giant tower in the playground (or am I?). There are simpler ways of leading your pupils into being bewitched by shape: ways which don't involve explaining to your head why you have had to call in the fire brigade to extract Dan from a pile of collapsed corrugated card. My hope is that by the end of this chapter you will be communing with ideas that underline that there is vastly more to geometry than simply knowing the names and properties of 2D and 3D shapes.

We cover 2D and 3D shapes in the primary curriculum, and it is vital that children understand the fundamental difference between these two: 2D shapes are flat and 3D shapes are solid. By flat, I mean that 2D shapes exist on a plane and therefore only really exist in pictorial representations and as the faces of 3D shapes. In fact, every shape that you can physically come into contact with is 3D. This can cause some problems as even those flat plastic 2D shapes lurking in your maths cupboard/drawer/box/pile are in fact 3D. 2D shapes cut out of card or paper are also 3D. Put simply, nothing that physically exists can be truly 'flat'. There is a very reasonable argument that, because of this, 2D shapes should be explored predominately through drawing, looking at pictorial representations and examining the faces of 3D shapes, so as not to further compound an already confusing concept.

In this chapter, you will find ideas that present 2D shapes using these approaches, but you will also find some activities that explore 2D shapes in a not entirely 'flat' manner. I know that for many this will be against the rules, but I feel that the benefits with some of these more tactile and physical approaches outweigh the potential pitfalls. Just make sure that you remind the children over and over that 2D shapes are flat and 3D shapes are solid.

Before we go any further, using the clues below, grab a piece of paper and draw the shape that I am thinking of:

It has four sides.

Opposite sides are equal.

Opposite sides are parallel.

Opposite angles are equal.

Write the name of the shape that you have drawn below it.

What shape have you got?

Well, the shape I was describing was a parallelogram. What? You drew a square? Or a rectangle? Or a rhombus? No, my parallelogram is different to the one you have drawn. But you didn't really get it wrong. You see, the shape I have described could be either a square, a rectangle, a rhombus or a parallelogram. It is quite clear how this could be a confusing and difficult task for a child, and not just because there is more than one possible answer.

First of all, shapes can vary hugely not just in terms of the differences between, say, an octagon and circle but also between different versions of the same shape, as there is more than one way to create an octagon. The second issue is that I asked you to draw the shape I was describing, therefore making an assumption that you possess the graphical skills and equipment to illustrate the shape. Did you use a ruler? How did you know to use a ruler? How did you ensure that the opposite sides and angles are equal? The third potential stumbling block was that there are several pieces of vocabulary that you need to understand in order to draw the shape correctly: sides, opposite, parallel, angle. Not only that, but if you did guess correctly and drew a parallelogram, how difficult is it to spell the word correctly?

Never fear, though. These are but tiny blips on an otherwise beautiful geometrical journey, and blips we can quickly clear up before we go on any further.

1. JUMPING TO CONCLUSIONS

Learning what is a rectangle and what is not a rectangle, or what is a triangle and what is not a triangle, is sometimes not as easy as it first appears.

> That one is a rectangle because it has four sides and the top bit is longer than the sides and it is red.

> Pete

Not all rectangles are red, but for Pete, at this stage of his learning, they are. This is because the box of assorted 2D shapes that his group had been sorting into different piles of shapes, only contained red rectangles, blue squares, green triangles and yellow circles. The rectangles were all also the same size, though the squares (which are, after all, just conformist rectangles) were half their size. Pete rapidly jumped to a conclusion based on the evidence with which he had been provided: he knew that rectangles had four sides and that they had two 'long' sides and two 'short' sides, and that all of the rectangles he had encountered in this task were red. He could have made other assumptions as well, such as squares not being a type of rectangle, as they were a different colour, and also that they are only half the size of rectangles. Jumping to conclusions, misconceptions, false generalisations – call them what you will – can be a real stumbling block to the development of a sound understanding of geometry.

This problem is not just limited to learning about the properties of shapes. One incredibly common misconception surrounds right angles:

Children often struggle to identify right angles when they are shown orientated in any way that is different to the way in which they are displayed in a pupil's first encounters when learning about squares or rectangles. With this in mind, it's important to expose children to as varied a set of examples as possible.

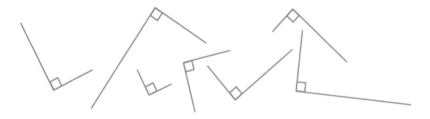

The idea of presenting children with lots of different examples is vital when learning about geometry, and it can take time. But you will find that if you grant your pupils sufficient time to explore differing presentations of shapes, their understanding of geometry will be all the richer.

So, what sort of activities help our pupils to become more shape and space savvy? A fantastic way to reinforce the concept that two shapes can have different proportions and still be the same type of shape is to introduce the idea of shape families. To do this, I give the pupils a 'family' of different variations of the same shape, with a few odd ones out, and ask them to find the shape that they think does not belong in the family.

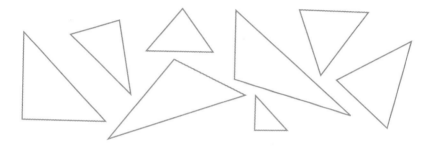

If you repeat this with several different shapes, you can get the pupils to then sort the shapes that do not belong into their correct families. Following this, get the pupils to justify their family groupings based on the properties of each shape family – for example, "These shapes all belong in this family because they all have three straight sides." (To extend this idea further, you can get the children to develop their own shape family posters or short picture books based on the 'Mr Men' series, complete with the reasons why they all have properties that make them part of the same family.)

Mr Isosceles Triangle and his family: Mrs Right Triangle, the Equilateral twins and Scalene the cat.

Another way to reinforce this idea is by creating groups of polygon creatures. The idea is simple: you provide the pupils with a wide range of polygons printed out on card, the pupils cut them out and sort them into groups (e.g. triangles, quadrilaterals, pentagons). Once they have their groups of shapes, they have to turn them into polygon creatures by adding features to them, with each group of shapes having different characteristics to create different types of creatures. You can do this activity quickly using felt-tip pens to annotate the polygons or take it a step further and break out some googly eyes or foam features.

Other approaches that work include asking the pupils to justify why something you have given to them or said to them is incorrect. For example, you could announce to the class, "Squares are the only shapes with four sides," or "All triangles have three sides of the same length," or "Hexagons are my favourite shape because I like shapes with eight sides," or "One of the things that make quadrilaterals different to other shapes is that they are the only shapes to have perpendicular lines." Alternatively, you can even give the children three statements about shapes, one of which contains a false statement. For example:

1   Rectangles always have a single set of parallel lines.

2   Pentagons have more sides than a parallelogram.

3   A right triangle contains a set of perpendicular lines.

This can also be accompanied by illustrated examples where the children have to spot what is wrong with the picture:

Polygon Pals

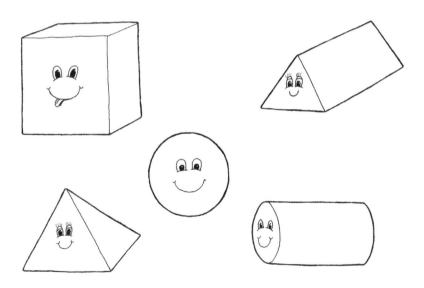

The reason this strategy works is because it is targeting something that children revel in: correcting the teacher. Despite a large proportion of the class being able to see immediately through this ruse, primary aged children take great pleasure in spotting any mistake you have made, even if you made it on purpose. This not only provides them with the opportunity to feel like a genius for outsmarting the teacher, but it also gives them something to brag about at home: "You'll never guess the mistake that Mr Tiley-Nunn made today ..."

Anyone can impress their parents: geometry homework

On the subject of giving them something to brag about at home, it is my view that the best type of homework activities are ones that allow the child to 'show off' something ace that they have learned at school that day. In the same way that children love catching you out when you make a mistake, they also revel in showing their parents something impressive. In primary mathematics, nothing says impressive quite like being able to demonstrate a formula. Even the most basic formula can seem impressive to the non-mathematician; the skilful substitution of letters for numbers and holds an almost mystical gravitas for adults too. Not only this, but when it comes to addressing false generalisations, formulae can be used to illustrate a point or to prove it, making them incredibly useful indeed.

The most ubiquitous formulae in geometry, and the most accessible, are those to do with the properties of circles. By Year 6, pupils should be able to, "illustrate and name parts of circles, including radius, diameter and circumference and know that the diameter is twice the radius".[2] But why stop there, when it only takes a touch more time to give them some nice little formulae to impress their granny with? Key to understanding the properties of circles is pi. When first introduced, pi embodies an entirely new concept for primary pupils, because it is represented by a symbol, π, and it may well be the first 'irrational number' they have encountered. Pi equals the ratio between the circumference and the diameter of a circle, but it is, in fact, only an approximation due to its irrational nature. The quest for calculating pi to as many places as possible is a big deal to some people and, as of December 2013, it had been calculated to over 12.1 trillion digits (so far). However, it is not just the calculation of pi that is taken seriously; the memorising of the order of the digits of pi is also an object of pride and competition among the elite of geeks, with Lu Chao currently holding the Guinness World Record for reciting pi to 67,890 places. Try challenging your class to memorise as many of the first 100 places as they can:

3.1415926535897932384626433832795028841971693993751058209749445923078164062862089986280348253421170679

Memorisation aside, the reason pi is so prized is the relationship it has with the circumference, diameter (and, therefore, the radius) of a circle. Due to its unwieldy and irrational nature, it is best to use the π function on a calculator when working with pi. With any circle, the circumference divided by the diameter will equal pi or:

2   Department for Education, *Mathematics Programs of Study: Key Stages 1 and 2. National curriculum in England* (September 2013). Available at: https://www.gov.uk/government/uploads/system/uploads/attachment_data/file/335158/PRIMARY_national_curriculum_-_Mathematics_220714.pdf, p. 44.

$$\frac{\text{Circumference}}{\text{Diameter}} = 3.141592 = \pi$$

This means that you can work out the circumference of a circle providing you know its diameter or radius. For instance, if you have a circle with a 10 m diameter then you can work out the circumference by calculating 10 m x π = 31.42 m (rounded to the nearest cm). It also means that if you know the circumference of circle then you can work out the diameter by dividing the circumference by pi. For example, if you have a circumference of 31.42 m then you can work out the diameter by calculating:

31.42 ÷ π = 10 m (rounded to the nearest cm)

Another useful formula involving pi is how to work out the area of a circle. This is most commonly calculated using the radius (half the diameter). The area of any given circle can be worked out using the formula:

$A = \pi r^2$

This is more easily remembered using the awful maths pun: 'Pie are squared … but more often than not they're round.'

For example, if a circle has a radius of 10 cm you can work out the area by calculating π x 10^2 which is the same as π x 100, and equals 314 cm^2 (rounded to the nearest cm^2).

Now, these formulae are interesting enough, but how are the kids going to use them to wow their pet gerbil, Stanley? Or their nan? By demonstrating them! But not in a boring paper and pen way – they will demonstrate them with real life examples. Set each child the challenge of seeing how close they can get to pi when they measure the circumference and diameter of five circular objects at home. Tell them that they will need a witness (e.g. parent, grandparent, sibling) to help them select the objects. Also, tell the children that they must make a prediction in front of the witness before they measure anything, and that every time they divide the circumference by the diameter the answer will be between 3 and 3.5. The children will need something to measure with, such as a flexible measuring tape or a ball of string and a ruler, as well as a calculator. All they need to do is measure the circumference by wrapping the tape or string carefully around the outer edge, then measure the diameter by placing the tape or string from one side to the other across what they estimate is the middle of the circle, and then divide the first measurement by the second one on a calculator. Simple! It works particularly well if the witness is a slightly younger sibling, because, in this case, they will be determined to prove their older brother or sister wrong. But if they measure it carefully, no matter what circular object is put in front of them, the answer will always prove their prediction.

Other relatively simple formulae that your more able primary geometricians can use to show off at home include the formula for working out the number of diagonals in a polygon:

number of sides (number of sides − 3) ÷ 2

Or:

$n (n − 3) ÷ 2$

For example, a hexagon has six sides; therefore, to work out the number of diagonals for a hexagon we can do the following:

6 (6 − 3) ÷ 2 which is (6 x 3) ÷ 2 which is 18 ÷ 2 which equals 9

Or for a pentagon (which has five sides):

$$5 (5 - 3) \div 2 = 5$$

Or for an icosagon (which has 20 sides):

$$20 (20 - 3) \div 2 = 170$$

Euler's formula, which describes a fundamental property of polyhedra is also a useful show off:

faces + vertices – edges = 2

Or:

$$F + V - E = 2$$

If you take a cube as an example, it has the following properties: six faces, eight vertices and twelve edges. If we apply Euler's formula to this we see:

$$6 + 8 - 12 = 2$$

This rule is the same for many solid shapes. So, how could your class use this one to impress at home? I tell the kids to go home and tell their parents that they have been learning about 3D shapes. They have been asked to fill in the missing numbers in a table (like the one opposite) of the properties of some common 3D shapes and they would like some help just to check that they are doing it correctly.

Shape	Faces	Vertices	Edges
Tetrahedron	4		6
Cube		8	12
Triangular prism	5	6	
Pentagonal prism	7	10	
Square pyramid		5	8
Icosahedron	20	12	

They start by working through some of the more basic shapes together, like a tetrahedron, a cube or triangular prism, before the child lays their trap for the unsuspecting parent. They challenge their parent to a race to fill in the last missing gap. The last space on the table is an icosahedron (a polyhedron with 20 faces), and it is best to set it up so the child is given the number of faces and the number of vertices, leaving them only to find out the number of edges. During the lesson preceding this homework, they will have looked at how Euler's formula can be manipulated to their advantage, so they know that to work out the number of edges all they need to do is subtract 2 from the sum of faces and vertices:

20 + 12 = 32 and 32 − 2 = 30

Many adults will not have encountered icosahedrons and will find it tricky to work out the number of edges by the common approaches of drawing it or picturing it in their heads. Imagine their surprise when their darling daughter or son gets the answer in a couple of seconds!

2. GRAPHICAL SKILLS

A drawing is simply a line going for a walk.

Paul Klee

I remember one of my art teachers saying this to me as a child and it being something that annoyed me: there was nothing 'simple' in drawing and I could barely get lines to stumble and crawl, let alone walk. I have already mentioned that I didn't much like maths as a child, but my dislike of it was as nothing compared to my hatred of art. Art was the one subject which I felt that I had truly irreconcilable differences with as a child. I dodged all arty activities as they would bring me out in hives. Drawing does not necessarily come easily to all children, and this doesn't only affect the child struggling to sketch a bowl of fruit. The study of geometry often relies heavily on graphical skills. As children progress in their learning of geometry they will be expected to use a range of different graphical tools: rulers, protractors, pairs of compasses. Learning how to use this equipment takes practice and can be really frustrating for young humans.

Geometry is a skill of the eyes and the hands as well as of the mind.

Jean Pedersen

From Year 2 onwards, children are expected to be able to draw 2D shapes using a pencil and ruler. Rulers are actually not easy things to use when you are 6 years of age. When asking children to use rulers, pairs of compasses or protractors, it is imperative that correct use is modelled by the teacher. The difficulty with modelling how to use this equipment is that it is quite small and therefore difficult for everyone in the class to see how you are doing it. Teachers therefore find themselves with the following options:

1   Demonstrate how to use the equipment by standing at the front of the class, optimistically hoping that all the children have phenomenal eyesight and can make out exactly what you are asking them to do.

2   Use large whiteboard versions of graphical tools to demonstrate what you mean. The trouble with these is that they very rarely look much like the graphical tools that the children will be using themselves.

3   Employ virtual versions of the graphical tools on an interactive white-board. Except, once again, these often do not resemble the tools that the children will be using and, in many cases, are manipulated in a different way.

4   Visit each table individually to explain how to use the tools correctly. This can take ages and may well leave you feeling like you have taken part in the annual musical tables competition.

5   Use a visualiser or webcam to demonstrate the correct technique using exactly the same equipment as the children.

My preferred approach is option 5, followed up by option 4. I cannot empha-sise enough just how useful a visualiser is for demonstrating graphical techniques that require accuracy. For those who have not used one, a visual-iser or document camera allows you to project images onto your whiteboard using your normal projector/computer/interactive whiteboard set-up. They range in price from thousands of pounds to the one that I have used for the past few years which cost less than £40. The key benefit of using one of these ace pieces of kit is that you can demonstrate skills using exactly the same paper or exercise book, exactly the same equipment and exactly the same technique as you want the pupils to use, and in real time. The camera also allows you to take still pictures of important steps in the process, so you can create a visual aide-memoire to be used (perhaps as a display item) at a later stage. If you put one thing on your wish list from the techno-fairies then make it a visualiser; it will be one of the best pieces of technology you will ever use.

One of the simplest ways to ensure that children develop a sound understanding of geometry, without them having to endure the stumbling blocks of poor graphical skills, is to make sure that they have plenty of opportunity to make shapes. Making shapes does not necessarily have to involve using a pencil, nor does it need to involve any questionable dance moves. However, it may require a bit of geometric rule breaking! A decent first port of call when first creating shapes is to see what shapes they can create from themselves. Children should be given the opportunity to make shapes with their fingers, limbs and bodies; on their own, in a pair or as part of a group. A great activity to try with your class is splitting them into pairs and giving them one minute to create as many different recognisable shapes as they can. What becomes apparent very quickly is that it is difficult to create shapes just using ourselves and that there must, somehow, be an easier way. Perhaps we should think about using some materials instead ...

Keeping in with the theme of variation, children should try to make shapes out of as many different things as possible. My favourite shape-building resources are straws (preferably art straws but drinking straws will do). These are my weapons of choice for a variety of reasons. First, they are easily adaptable as they can be cut into different sizes and connected together to create the required shape. Second, they are colourful, eye-catching and non-threatening. Finally, they're cheap. There are many ways you can use straws to make shapes, and the obvious approach of simply providing children with a number of straws and asking them to connect them together to form shapes is a fairly good one. But for something a bit different, I like to incorporate a piece of string. It works something like this:

1   Cut several straws into equal lengths, ideally the size of the piece at the top just before the straw bends.

2   Cut the string into 30 cm lengths.

3   Split the class into pairs and give each pair ten sections of straw and one length of string.

4   The pupils thread the sections of straw onto the string.

Your pupils now have one of the most sophisticated pieces of 2D shape making apparatus known to man, the PolyStraw! The benefits of this piece of apparatus is that the children can create all of the polygons from triangles though to decagons and ever onwards by simply manipulating the sections of straw on the string. Not only can they create these polygons, but they can also create different variations of the same polygon.

This experimentation provides the perfect context in which to question and extend the pupils' knowledge of 3D shapes. To really get their minds buzzing, how about asking them what they notice when they move, in sequence, through the regular polygons from triangle to quadrilateral to pentagon to hexagon to heptagon to octagon to nonagon to decagon? What would happen if we added another 20 sections of the straws? As the number of sides (sections of straw) increase, would the shape become more like a circle?

To demonstrate this further, you can supersize the apparatus by replacing straws and string with cardboard kitchen roll tubes and a length of rope. Repeat the process, starting with an equilateral triangle made from three cardboard tubes, and increase the number of sides one by one. As more and more sides are added, the shape becomes more obviously circular. This is great for addressing the misconception that a circle is a one sided shape; after all, surely it should become less like a circle as the number of sides increase, rather than more like one? The circle, you see, is not actually a polygon because it doesn't have any straight sides, but is, in fact, a curve that remains the same distance away from the centre. Another excellent way of showing this is using an interactive shape resource such as the Interactive Polygons page on the superb mathisfun.com website.[3]

Another fantastic resource for creating shapes are pin boards and elastic bands. In order to create shapes you simply stretch an elastic band over the pins. You can do tons of great activities with them, but they are at their best when encouraging the children to investigate a more open ended question. One such exercise is to ask the pupils to see how many different triangles they can create on a single pin board. This is a super way of introducing the terms 'congruent' and' similar', as children will almost certainly create tri-angles that are the same as previous ones, but they will have been rotated or translated (congruent), or they will have the same shape as previous ones but have been either enlarged or reduced in size (similar).

Interestingly, while I was delivering a course last year, a teacher with over 20 years' experience told me he was no longer allowed to use pin boards and elastic bands in maths lessons for health and safety reasons! I could barely believe it, until another teacher said the same thing had happened at her school, and that they now had to use isometric (dotty) paper to simulate pin board activities. I am reminded of a section in the first book of this series, by the editor of this one, about health and safety:

Stanley knives and swimming pools apart, ignore anything else you are told about health and safety. Managers who are liable to use the phrase 'health and safety', a pejorative and superior sneer on their lips, and who do not have even a Northamptonian mum's idea of biting, satirical humour coursing through them as they utter the phrase, are doing so in order to hide the fact that they are, in all other areas, clueless. They are, in fact, on their fourth 'sideways' promotion having shown over the path of many years in the profession that they are not capable of running a bunk up in

---

3   See http://www.mathsisfun.com/geometry/polygons-interactive.html.

a brothel, let alone a special needs section. 'Health and safety' is the preserve of the bore, and will stop you from standing on desks, kids from standing on chairs and the whole class from piling those chairs up in the corner of the room and pretending you are all in a nuclear bunker. Spurn it as you would a rabid dog.[4]

If your school is being ridiculous and risk averse to an extent that is out of proportion to the danger, then my advice would be to completely ignore them and carry on. Pin boards are not dangerous! In fact, go one step further with the following activity. Split the children into pairs and give each pair either a ball of string or a long length of rope. Before you go any further, make sure you give the children a short safety briefing about how string, when wound tightly around a person's neck, can cause both harm and distress. The likelihood of this happening is incredibly minimal, but it's best to brief the pupils anyway, for both their protection and your own. Next, in the same way that we got the children to make shapes out of themselves earlier, we ask each pair to create as many shapes as possible with the string forming the sides and themselves forming the points or vertices. It won't take most of them more than a minute to realise that there is a limit to the number of shapes you can make when there are only two of you. This is an excellent way of demonstrating the whole point of the vertex; it allows a one-dimensional line to change into a 2D shape.

Following this, combine the children into ever increasing group sizes – pairs to fours, fours to eights and so on – until you have the whole class in one massed group. The result of this should be that the more vertices (children) they have, the more shapes they can make, as they can create a greater number of sides. Ask the children to use this information to produce a statement that sums up the relationship between vertices and sides.

---

4   Phil Beadle, *How to Teach* (Carmarthen: Crown House Publishing, 2010), pp. 76–77.

The possibilities of a ball of string or a length of rope don't stop there, though. I'm not suggesting that you tie Mitchell to the chair to stop him bouncing around the class, as this is unlikely to teach the class anything about geometry and, besides, management quite rightly tend to frown on that sort of thing. What I am thinking of is using string or rope for an introduction to plotting shapes as coordinates on a plane.

Earlier on, I suggested that you paint a large 10 x 10 grid on the floor of your playground. This grid can be an incredible resource for demonstrating coordinates. First of all, children need to know how to read coordinates – the horizontal coordinate first and then the vertical coordinate (or, as I was taught it, 'along the corridor and up the stairs'). Once you have reminded the children of how to read coordinates, label each axis from 1 to 10, with the numbers written on mini whiteboards. Next, ask each member of the class to stand at a point on the grid. When all the children are in position, call out the coordinates for where one of the children is standing. The child who is at that point then leaves the grid and it is their turn to call out the coordinates of another child, who then also leaves the grid and calls out another pair of coordinates. Keep this activity moving at a good pace until you have only three children left. Provided you haven't been particularly unlucky, and been left with the three remaining children standing in a line, they should be forming a triangular shape. Ask the children, "Can anyone spot a shape on the grid?" Some will be able to spot it at this stage but some will not. So, what you do next is to unwind some string between the points (children) left on the grid. Explain to the children that placing shapes on a grid makes it easier to describe their size and position.

Experiment with creating different shapes by giving groups of children various shapes to make on the grid and asking the rest of the class to note down the coordinates for each point. From here, you can use the grid to demonstrate translations, by asking children to make a shape and then all stepping two squares right and the one square down. You can also show reflections of a shape by placing a line of symmetry through the grid (I use a red piece of rope for this) and asking one group of children to make a shape on one side of the line and another group to mirror it on the other side. If you want to extend this even further, you can look at rotations, by asking the pupils to rotate around the point where one child is standing, and even resizing shapes, by asking pupils to move to take a certain number of steps backwards or forwards.

When it comes to the graphical skills required in the teaching of primary geometry, few things cause more difficulty for kids than measuring angles. Protractors can be very difficult pieces of kit to use properly and should not really be anywhere near the classroom when children have their first taught experiences of angles, because before children start measuring angles they should be recognising them. The national curriculum doesn't expect children to start using protractors until around Year 5, so resist the temptation to introduce them until the children really understand what an angle is and are pretty good at recognising whether they are acute, right or obtuse.

One tool that can help children to recognise different versions of angles is what I call an Anglesaurus:

This simple device can be created by giving each child a circle of thin card and asking them to fold it into quarters. They then cut out one of the quarters to leave behind a three-quarter circle, and then decorate them so that they look like dinosaurs. The Anglesaurus works as a very simple angle gauge. The children can place the Anglesaurus against an angle and if it fits entirely inside the mouth then the angle must be an acute angle. If the angle aligns itself with the mouth of Anglesaurus then it must be a right angle. If the angle does not fit inside the mouth then it is obtuse. You don't have to use the dinosaur theme for this and I am sure that other teachers make similar tools, but the Anglesaurus really engages younger children in their quest to recognise the key varieties of angles.

Angle work in primary school tends to involve working through measuring the angles of vast and interminable quantities of boring shapes. This is important because, as with all graphical skills, measuring angles requires practice. However, this must not be the only experience that children have of measuring angles because this activity is blander and more boring than beige itself. It doesn't take much effort or thought to give the pupils some far more interesting angles to measure. As I have already alluded to, my drawing skills leave something to be desired, but I am borderline competent with stick figures. Most children are too and, what is more, stick figures can be used as a great opportunity for pupils to practise using a ruler accurately. To start with, just get them to draw a single stick figure in any pose that they like, ensuring rulers are used without exception.

Once they have drawn their stick figure, each child should swap with some-one else and measure as many angles as possible on the other pupil's stick person: the angle of his armpit, the angle at his ankle where the foot meets the leg. Once they have completed this, the next challenge is to draw a whole stick figure scene in about five minutes flat. The only rule is that everything they draw must be formed from straight lines and, therefore, must be done using a ruler. Encourage the kids to think as broadly as possible, and you will no doubt end up with some incredibly interesting stick figure narratives. I've had everything from stick figures at a disco, to stick figures on *Britain's Got Talent*, to stick figures fighting off stick space-bat-angel-dragons. Five min-utes is all it takes to have something far more interesting to measure with a protractor than a load of dull, disembodied shapes. It doesn't even have to be stick figures – how about continuing the dinosaur theme from the Anglesaurus and having stick dinos in some dramatic tableaux that pupils can measure the angles from?

BUT, SIR, WHERE ARE WE GOING TO FIND A PROTRACTOR BIG ENOUGH TO MEASURE THAT TREE!?

What have a kite, two shoes, Mitch the cat, a ladder, a bucket of pink paint, a duck, a chair, a friend's bicycle, a kitchen sink, a front door, a family car, a milkman, an orang-utan, a small boat, a big boat, a rhinoceros, a long distance lorry, the house across the street, a lighthouse and a curious whale got in common? The answer is that they all got 'stuck', which is not such a bad thing, especially when we are talking about the ace book, *Stuck*, by Oliver Jeffers.[5] This book, like most of his work, is pure genius and is one of my favourite picture books. However, my use of it in the mathematics classroom came about as part of a challenge from a colleague. I had been gushing about maths being the most important subject, and how it was all around us in everything that we see and do. Her response was that she wanted me to use something non-mathsy (of her choice) to teach a great maths lesson and, what's more, she wanted to observe it as well. The next day, I arrived at school to find a copy of *Stuck* on my desk with a sticky note reading, 'Good luck!' stuck to the front of it. I flicked through the pages and found the standard Oliver Jeffers formula of incredible illustrations with an infant-like quality to them, coupled with a simple, repetitive but well thought out storyline. Floyd gets his favourite kite stuck up the tree and in order to get it down he starts to chuck things at it, which also become stuck in the tree. He perseveres. But just when you think he has got the right idea, he ends up repeating the same mistake by chucking another item into the tree. By the time the curious whale is stuck in the tree, you are sure that Floyd will remain hopelessly stuck and will never get to fly his favourite kite again. Well, where is the maths in that?

---

5   Oliver Jeffers, *Stuck* (London: HarperCollins Children's Books, 2011).

I wasn't sure myself until I turned to the page where the whale had just been hurled into the tree, which reads, "And they all got stuck!" This page features a double-page spread with Floyd standing at the base of the tree contemplating how he is going to get all the stuck items down. I lingered on this page for a while. Angles! I could use it for angles! But how spicy could I make it? The options I had were:

- Korma. Use the story as an introduction into the importance of angles: if Floyd had known about angles, he might have been more successful at throwing things into the tree. Followed by using a generic angle measurement exercise to drill protractor skills.

- Tikka Masala. Read the story and draw my own version of the 'And they all got stuck!' page and ask pupils to draw lines from Floyd to an object and from the tree to Floyd to create angles for the children to measure using a protractor.

- Vindaloo. Similar to above but with additional chilli!

I went for a hefty portion of Vindaloo! I started the lesson by reading the book with the class to the point where the whale gets stuck. It was at this point that things got spicy, as the children were told that they could help Floyd out if they went out to the playground. During the previous lesson, I had been lucky enough to have a rare planning, preparation and assessment period and had used it to adorn one of the trees with several items, including a kite, a pair of shoes, a bucket, a toy cat, a toy duck, a toy orang-utan, a school chair and my bike. The chilli had the desired effect as the children were left awestruck and reeling by the sight of the tree festooned by objects.

I explained that we were going to measure the angles Floyd needed to throw things at in order to knock the items down from the tree. This lot knew how to measure angles and could use a protractor, but they couldn't work out how they were going to use a protractor for this! I revealed to them that we weren't actually going to use protractors, and dished out clinometers.

Sometimes called angle guns, you are likely to have at least one of these knocking about in school somewhere (they tend to be used solely for geography field trips), but if you don't have one, they cost peanuts so it's well worth investing in a few. Clinometers work by holding them outstretched in your hand and pointing at the desired target in a similar way to a pistol. You press the trigger and it releases the stopper on a weighted protractor which swings around to give the angle between your hand and the target. Simple! We were fortunate enough to have a small set of clinometers, so the children were split into groups and began working their way around the tree, which I had placed cones around to ensure that a safe and uniform distance was maintained while the children were measuring the angles of the different items that were stuck in the tree.

Back in the classroom, the children – still buzzing from the tree activity – were given a sheet with a picture of Floyd and the tree, along with some of the objects that I couldn't find to put in my tree. They measured the angle of these objects from Floyd using a protractor and marked them on their sheet. Following this, some pupils moved on to mapping the objects we had measured outside onto their sheet using the angle measurement they had taken earlier with the clinometers.

I loved teaching this lesson and the children loved being part of it. However, a word to the wise: lessons this spicy can be bad for your health. I hope that by now this book has inspired you to try some more creative approaches to teaching primary mathematics, but not every lesson can be like this, nor should it be. You have to plan, deliver and assess a huge number of lessons every week, and if you try to deliver each lesson with this level of spice you will be dead before the end of half-term. If we look back at the less spicy options I could have chosen for this lesson, then both the Korma and Tikka Masala activities would have been a substantial improvement on just turning to page 115 in the textbook, and would have taken significantly less time to plan than the full Vindaloo. But it is worth breaking out the really heavy seasoning once in a while!

3. VOCABULARY

Polygon, polyhedron, vertex, face, edge, diagonal, regular, irregular, concave, convex, congruent, similar, parallel, perpendicular, dodecahedron ... the list of vocabulary that children encounter during the study of geometry is seemingly near endless. This is actually a good thing because children love learning new words, particularly if it sounds properly 'mathsy'. It is not the vocabulary itself that holds them back on occasion, but the spelling of it. And though I would never mark a child down for incorrect spelling of mathematical terminology, I do expect them to use the terms in both discussion and written work. One of the ways that I suggest developing sound mathematical vocabulary is through the use of a maths dictionary. There are tons of these on the market and some are really good. However, none are anywhere near as good as ones that the children have made themselves. In the same way that children often have their own personal dictionaries to jot down difficult spellings in literacy lessons, pupils should also be creating their own maths dictionary when learning new terms. One of the most important elements of any pupil-made maths dictionary is the way in which it is presented. For maximum effect, ensure the following guidelines are followed:

- Entries in the dictionary should be spaced out. In order to achieve this, you should refrain from using the tiny (203 x 100 mm) vocabulary exercise books that probably clutter the stationery cupboard at your school. Give the pupils a decent sized exercise book in which they can set out their work neatly rather than giving them a piece of kit which requires that they write in tiny handwriting, desperately failing to cram it all in.

- Insist on the neatest possible presentation in this book. If it is untidy, it will not get looked at very often.

- Insist that the pupils include illustrated examples wherever appropriate. It is often easier to explain mathematical concepts with a combination of worked examples, pictures and words than it is with words alone. Sometimes, it helps to have some pre-prepared examples they can stick into their book when you know you will be introducing some new terms.

- Ensure that maths dictionaries get passed on. There is little point in setting up a maths dictionary for one year of their primary schooling if it is not used in subsequent years. Insist that your colleagues continue using the maths dictionaries with the kids long after they have left you.

Another great way to improve children's mathematical vocabulary is to ensure that you plan for plenty of activities that involve discussion. In terms of geometry, there are several activities that I always incorporate into my teaching to get my pupils nattering about shapes. A favourite of mine is a variation on the popular board game of Guess Who? In my version, children are put into pairs and given three identical packs of nine laminated cards. Each child takes one of the packs of cards and the third pack of cards is placed in the middle. On each card there is a different shape, so that each child has a set of nine shapes that are identical to their partner's. Each child then takes a card from the third set in the middle; this is the card that their partner is trying to guess.

The children take it in turns to ask each other questions that can only be answered yes or no – for example, "Does your shape have more than four sides?" or "Is your shape a quadrilateral?" As the children ask each other questions they should be able to eliminate possible options, placing cards that their partner could not possibly have in a pile face down on the desk. Once they feel that they know what card their partner has got, they make an educated guess. A good way to ensure that children do not simply try to guess every turn or straight away is to impose a miss-a-turn penalty for when they guess incorrectly. This game can be scaled up in difficulty by adding more cards or including several shapes that are similar – for example, several mildly different quadrilaterals. Alternatively, you can introduce finer rules, such as not allowing questions about the number of sides.

Games that involve partners sitting back to back can be an excellent context for promoting discussion of shapes. One of my favourites is Play-Doh Polyhedron.[6] In this game, the children take it in turns to be either the person making and describing a polyhedron or the person using their description to make an unseen polyhedron. The maker quickly knocks up a polyhedron out of a ball of modelling clay, making sure they keep their shape secret from their partner. Once they have made their chosen shape, they must describe their shape to their partner who will try to replicate it out of their ball of clay by following their instructions. This game is quite tricky to start with, but is a fantastic way of getting children to use key vocabulary.

Puzzles, like games, are great for getting children chatting about shapes. Of all the shape puzzles, tangrams are my favourite. This ancient Chinese puzzle consists of seven pieces or tans: a parallelogram, two large isosceles triangles, one medium-sized isosceles triangles, two small isosceles triangles and a small square. The tans all fit together to create a square. They are readily available, but can just as easily be made from a square piece of paper or card. Traditionally, the tans are used to form figures, such as animals, and then asking someone to copy the shape you have made. *Grandfather Tang's Story* by Ann Tompert is 'A Tale Told with Tangrams', in which Little Soo is told a story by grandfather about two fox fairies.[7] The fox fairies have magical powers which enable them to change into different kinds of animals, and the story tells the tale of how they compete with each other. Each different animal that they change into is illustrated in the book with an image of the tangram of that particular animal. The tangrams in the story can be used for another back-to-back paired activity, with one child making one of the tangrams from the story and describing the shape and position of each tan so their partner can copy it. To extend this further, the children can create

---

6   A polyhedron is a three-dimensional solid which has flat faces, straight edges and sharp corners.

7   Ann Tompert, *Grandfather Tang's Story: A Tale Told with Tangrams* (New York: Crown Publications/Dragonfly Books, 1998).

their own tangrams and even use these as a resource with which to write or tell their own tangram tale.

BRINGING SHAPE, SPACE AND POSITION TO LIFE

You can build understanding of how geometry works in real life through looking at architecture and engineering:

'It looks like frog spawn bubbling out of the ground' – Dan

Dan's right. It does (kind of). This was one child's response to seeing a picture of the Rainforest Biome at the Eden Project. This quite incredible geodesic structure covers an area of 15,590m² is 50m high and is made of a steel skeleton of 502 hexagons of varying sizes, which hold panels made of ethylene tetrafluoroethylene. It is a simply stunning structure that begs to be gawped at. To my mind, there is not a better way to explore both 2D and 3D shapes than through the architecture and engineering of buildings and structures. Using architecture to teach shape, space and measure is a fantastic way of bringing geometry, and therefore primary mathematics, to life.

Buildings are real, they are readily available and they provide an excellent context for transitioning between 2D and 3D shapes. Structures can also be unique, irregular and fascinating, thereby providing culturally rich opportunities to discuss shape in detail that reinforces, but also goes beyond, subject specific vocabulary.

Where to start? Well, before you go anywhere with buildings it is worth mentioning that the children will need to have at least a basic understanding of the main 2D and 3D shapes and their properties. I often start looking at buildings with pupils when I want to make links between 2D shapes and how they manifest themselves as faces on 3D shapes. Jenny Broom's *Walk This World* (illustrated by Lotta Nieminen) is an incredible picture book which explores the illustrations of cityscapes from around the world in the most vibrant and colourful way imaginable.[8] I like to start off with the double-page spread showing London, and simply ask the children to spot as many shapes as they can. We then compare the shapes that we found in this illustration with the other illustrations in the book of different cityscapes from around the world. We then discuss which shapes we see most often and which shapes we don't see.

I then ask the children, "So, are all these cities made out of 2D shapes in real life?" This question is perhaps trickier than it first appears as, although all of the illustrations show the cityscapes of made up of 2D shapes, the children already know that physical objects are always 3D. However, I then ask, "Aren't 3D shapes made out of 2D shapes?" The ensuing discussion leads

---

8   Jenny Broom, *Walk This World* (Somerville, MA: Big Picture Press, 2013).

nicely into one of the best things about using buildings to study shape: they allow you to move from 2D to 3D in a meaningful and easily contextualised way. The best way to look at the shapes in buildings is to get outside and go for a walk around your nearest town or city. It goes without saying that it is not quite as simple as putting on your coats and walking out the front gates. Any school trip – be it a walk down the road or trekking in the foothills of the Himalayas – requires a certain amount of paperwork and box ticking. However, it is worth gritting your teeth and persevering.

Not so long ago, I took my class to London for the day and we went on a river cruise on the Thames, as we had been studying London as a settlement and were focusing on the role the Thames had played in the historical development of the city. During the hour-and-a-half trip along the river, the pupils were tasked with creating quick line sketches and taking photos of buildings and structures that interested them. The children were wowed by the modern glass structures juxtaposed with reminders of London's rich and varied past lining the banks of the river. Some of the sketches they created were excellent, but they paled compared to the quality of discussion the buildings provoked. From marvelling at the sheer scale of the iconic buildings around them, to asking how they managed to get the Gherkin to curve, to estimating how many triangles there were on the London Eye, to how many different shapes there were in the Southbank Centre or whether it was all just one shape, the children were buzzing. For all of the potential hassle of taking school trips, the learning was worth it.

When we got back to the classroom, the children looked through the photos they had taken. One of the best things about the rise of mobile devices is that we often have a camera close to hand, and this means that it is easier than ever to collect images for use in the classroom. We trawled through the photos we had taken, picking out the buildings and structures that had caught our eye. From the sweeping rhomboid panes of glass on the Gherkin, to the magnificent dome perched on top of St Paul's Cathedral, to the incredible framework of the Millennium Bridge, the children found plenty of examples to discuss.

Sarah came up with a corker of a question: "Who decides to make a building in a certain way?" and then commented on how so many of the buildings along the Thames were radically different in size, shape and in the materials used. Several of the children came to the agreement that it was builders who decided how a building was going to be built, until Rachel pointed out, "Builders just build the building. They don't decide how it is going to be built. The person who decides what a building will look like is called an architect." I asked the class whether they had heard of an architect before and most either shook their head from side to side or looked at me in a puzzled manner.

So, we started the next lesson with a great book by Andrea Beaty called *Iggy Peck: Architect*[9] – a story about a vastly talented little boy who wants nothing more from life than to design incredible structures. The children were then asked if they thought being an architect would be a good job. Most had never considered this as up until yesterday they didn't know they existed. James asked, "Can I be an architect and a footballer?" Clare wanted to know how much architects get paid. Given a minute or two to discuss in pairs, most of the children decided that it would be quite a cool job. Mo seemed to provide the most convincing argument for the profession: "Well, I love playing with my Lego and I've asked for some K'NEX for my birthday, so I guess being an architect would be like a giant, real version of playing with Lego."

Using school trips in which you deploy architecture to sell geometry is a complete winner. It is estimated that there are about 70 Lego bricks for every inhabitant of the world, that seven Lego sets are sold every second and that the number of Lego bricks sold in a year would encircle the earth five times over. Furthermore, if you stacked all of the Lego bricks ever produced

---

9   Andrea Beaty, *Iggy Peck: Architect* (New York: Harry N. Abrams, Inc., 2007).

on top of each other it would connect the earth and the moon ten times over.[10] The success and prominence of toys like Lego does not seem to falter. The reason for this can be boiled down to the simple fact that there is an enormous joy in building things.

Our trip on the Thames set the ball rolling on a lovely project where the pupils were tasked with designing a new building for the school. The children started by using the pictures they had taken during their trip and by searching for images of buildings and structures on the internet to create a mood board for their designs. We spent a single lesson on this, and did not waste time using paint charts to identify exactly the right shade of lavender! Our focus was instead on looking at what sort of shapes the children wanted to incorporate into their design.

The next lesson started with a run-through of the success criteria for the project. The children were required to create a model of their building design in a medium of their choice. They were asked to produce a short rationale or pitch explaining their design and were going to have to present their work at the end of the week. Having noticed from their mood boards that the majority of the children had included designs that incorporated triangular shapes, such as the Eiffel Tower, the roof of the British Museum, the concourse at King's Cross station and the archway of Wembley, I decided that we would focus on triangles before going any further.

The children were asked to come up with hypotheses as to why triangles are used so often in construction. Most suggested that it was because they looked nice; some suggested it saved money because triangles had one side less than squares and rectangles, meaning that it would cost less to build a structure out of triangles; some were clever enough to voice the thought that it must be something to do with triangles being easy or good

---

10 Lego statistics sourced from Lewis Dean, Lego Craze: Adults Go AFOL for Iconic Bricks, *International Business Times* (20 February 2014). Available at: http://www.ibtimes.co.uk/lego-craze-adults-go-afol-iconic-bricks-1437212.

to build with. With the children unsure as to why triangles were prevalent in so many structures, the clear thing to do was to build something with triangles ourselves.

The children decided that they wanted to build with some rectangles as well, to compare the triangles against, as these were the next most popular shape in the buildings that we had seen. We constructed equilateral triangles and squares by taping art straws together with sticky tape. Did the triangles look any better than the squares? Some thought so. Others did not agree. Would it cost less to build a wall out of triangles than squares? Some thought so, but then Brendan suggested that in order to have triangles that covered the same area as a square we would in fact need to use five straws rather than four – meaning it could cost more. So, the reason for triangles being chosen as a building structure must have something to do with them being better to build with.

We discussed what the key things were that we look for in a building. Following the suggestions that it should have lots of space, look nice and be comfortable to be inside, Emma joked that it shouldn't fall down. Everyone laughed. But then they second guessed their laughter because actually Emma had hit on something that was clearly quite important. The children decided that it must be something to do with how strong triangles are. And they were right: triangles are often used in the construction of buildings because of their strength. This is quite easily demonstrated with the art straw models that the children made by applying pressure with their fingertips to one of the vertices. With very little pressure, the square begins to fold over and semi-collapse into a version of a parallelogram, yet the triangle holds its shape when even more pressure is applied[11].

---

11   See http://www.rogersconnection.com/triangles/

You could look at this idea in more detail by investigating other structures around you that contain triangles (e.g. playground equipment), by building bridges and making 3D shapes and dens out of sticks in the playground.

We followed up our look at triangles with a twist on the Marshmallow Challenge. This challenge has become a mainstay of team-building sessions within corporate institutions but, as Tom Wujec says in his TED talk, often the most successful participants in this challenge are actually children.[12] The original challenge has some strict rules, with teams required to build the tallest free-standing structure out of 20 sticks of spaghetti, one yard of sticky tape, one yard of string and one marshmallow. They are allowed only 18 minutes to construct this, and the marshmallow must be on the very top!

For my version, I do away with the string and sticky tape but give each group an entire bag of marshmallows and an entire pack of spaghetti. I ask the children to use the marshmallows to link their spaghetti structure together, which poses some interesting questions for the children: should they use more than one strand of spaghetti to make each strut? How wide should the base be? What shapes should they try to incorporate into their design? Is it better to use the sticks of spaghetti and the marshmallows whole or should they try to split them into smaller pieces? This activity is a great way for the children put into practice some of their design ideas before settling on a structure for their final building project: the school building.

The lessons that followed during the rest of week consisted of the children designing and building their model structures. Some used Lego, some used lollipop sticks, some straws, some used Geomags and some used junk material, like cardboard tubes and food packaging. This was a far from easy process and there was frustration, disappointment and even a few tears along the way. However, all the children persevered and made a structure of which they were proud.

---

12   See http://marshmallowchallenge.com/TED_Talk.html.

In the final session of the week, the children were required to present their structures to the head, explaining their design and answering any questions that he had about their proposed building. The head was amazed by the results and so were the children. They not only took pride in what they had created and achieved, but also in the work of their peers. When asked afterwards if they thought being an architect was a good job, the answer was a resounding YES!

POSITION AND DIRECTION

As a child, I remember loving the Michael Rosen poem, *We're Going on a Bear Hunt*. It tells the tale of a family out on a bear hunt, who are confronted by several obstacles. From long, wavy grass to a narrow, gloomy cave, the family deals with these problems before being confronted by what they came hunting for: a bear! The book is ubiquitous for good reason: it is about an adventure, it is easy to relate to and it is fun to read aloud (especially with actions). I have used the poem many times in the classroom, but my most successful use of it was not in literacy classes, but as part of a maths lesson on position and direction.

Having worked on the poem as part of our literacy work, the children were presented with a sheet of A3 paper containing a grid of 2 cm squares that I had drawn in with a marker pen. The children were also given an envelope containing small laminated images of the obstacles that the family encountered on their bear hunt. They were told that they would be creating a map of the family's adventure by placing the laminated images on their square grid, and were asked to sequence the order in which the family tackled each obstacle, and then to place each obstacle on the square of their choice on the grid.

Once the children had ordered their obstacles, they were each given a little Lego man and told to 'walk' him from obstacle to obstacle. They were then asked if there was more than one possible route the Lego man could take. Why did they choose their preferred route? After this, the children were asked to demonstrate their route to another person by walking their Lego man through it, only this time they had to describe what the Lego man was doing using language to describe the direction (e.g. two squares forwards, rotate a quarter turn clockwise).

To finish, the children were given a double-sided grid. On one side the grid was blank and on the other side a pre-prepared route had been plotted through the obstacles. In pairs, they took it in turns to describe the route that their partner would need to take to get round all the obstacles, while the other partner mapped out the route on the blank grid. The first time that I tried this lesson it went swimmingly and, although I could not claim that it has gone quite so well every time, the children gained a far more detailed understanding of position and direction than if we had turned to page 93 in the textbook.

Practically the entire position and direction element of the primary maths curriculum can be covered through looking at stories involving journeys. You can explore specific vocabulary to describe position, direction and move-ment; you can sequence, order and arrange mathematical objects; you can explore turnings and angles; you can plot points and use coordinates on a grid; and you can describe translations. Not only this, but you can also address other parts of the primary mathematics curriculum such as length and time.

One of the keys to using stories about journeys to teach geometry is get-ting the children excited about maps. Maps have a magical quality; they can guide you towards hidden treasure and they can take you on incredible adventures. A great book to start your adventures with is *Henry's Map* by

David Elliot.[13] This tells the story of a meticulous little pig who likes things 'just so', and decides to draw a map of exactly where everything should be placed on the disorganised farm where he lives. Another super book is *Maps* by Aleksandra and Daniel Mizielinski.[14] It is very much like an atlas, but one that contains maps illustrated with so much detail about the people, customs, wildlife and history of each country that each map tells a story in its own: from a nod to the absurd with the 'alien(s)' at Roswell and King Kong at the Empire State Building on the USA map, to the references to Mayan culture in the map of Mexico, to the fact that the only noticeable landmarks in East Anglia are wheat, sugar beets and potatoes. The key to both of these books is that they use illustrated maps, where the basic outline is combined with small pictures to show important features. This is vital for using journeys to teach geometry, as these places provide reference points around which position and direction can be described. They are also easy to understand and far more appealing to the eyes of primary pupils than your average Ordnance Survey map. Children should be provided with plenty of opportunities to draw their own maps and to become confident in using the correct language to describe and guide people around their maps.

There is no shortage of children's books about journeys, but two that I like using are:

- *The Journey Home* by Frann Preston-Gannon.[15] The story of a Polar Bear who sets off on an adventure across the sea to find a new home, following the melting of the Polar ice he lives on. He meets friends along the way who also need to find a new home. I like this one because of the potential provided by the different islands. This provides a great context for learning about cardinal compass directions.

---

13 David Elliot, *Henry's Map* (New York: Philomel/Penguin, 2013).
14 Aleksandra Mizielinska and Daniel Mizielinski, *Maps* (Somerville, MA: Big Picture Press, 2013).
15 Frann Preston-Gannon, *The Journey Home* (London: Anova/Pavilion Children's Book, 2012).

• *Anno's Journey* by Mitsumasa Anno.[16] Despite not having any words, this stunning book comprises of beautiful pictures that tell the tale of a man and his journey through northern Europe on horseback. With more than a hint of 'Where's Wally?' about it, the children are instantly drawn in as they first look for Anno on each page, but often find more interesting and amusing details as Anno finds himself surrounded by scenes from famous examples of art, literature and folklore. This is a great book to use, as each double-page spread follows on from the last one, so it provides a challenging (but achievable) context for drawing a map of Anno's route. This is a difficult task, but older children relish mapping out the villages and countryside that Anno passes through.

These books, like so many others, provide a perfect starting point for delivering parts of the geometry curriculum. Having hooked the children's interest with a story, you have the perfect context for extended work on mapping and journeys. The links to other areas of mathematics and other subject areas are numerous: measurement of distances, scale and proportion, perimeter and area, calculation strategies required for problem-solving, both human and physical geography, storytelling and writing, technical drawing and modern foreign languages. With this in mind, I usually try to set aside some curriculum time for a more expansive piece of work on journeys, and I am always on the look-out for new ideas.

I recall a particularly interesting continuing professional development session with the editor of this very book in which we were shown a series of pictures in the form of a slideshow and asked to note down our emotional response to the images. I loved this idea and felt that it was ripe for a maths mash-up. My class were learning about coordinates and compass points at the time, so I went into the next lesson armed with nothing more than a pile of grids printed onto A3 and two simple slideshows on a USB stick. The class were told that they were going to see slideshows of pictures that I

---

16 Mitsumasa Anno, *Anno's Journey* (New York: Philomel, 1977).

had taken while I had been travelling around two very different islands and that, following the slide show, they were going to draw an illustrated map of what they thought one of the two islands looked like. The reason for using two separate islands is that it allows for comparison and contrast between the two different places; thereby providing more to discuss and think about during the mapping phase.

One of the slideshows contained images of ultra-modern architecture, bustling streets, bright lights; effectively a capitalist's dream, something like a cross between Macau and Dubai. The other slideshow contained images of rolling hills, pine-edged deserted beaches, quaint market towns and a field full of sheep; think Norfolk with hills. Once the children had viewed both slideshows, they were given the opportunity to find out more about each island to help them with mapping it out. In pairs, they had to come up with one question that they would like to ask an inhabitant of each island, played by myself with a daft moustache for one inhabitant followed by a dodgy blonde wig for the other. Although the odd question along the lines of, "What do you have for breakfast on your island?" is asked, most pairs come up with excellent questions like:

- What is the most famous thing on your island?

- How big is your island?

- What is your favourite thing about living on your island?

- How many people live on your island?

- What shape is your island?

Following the questions, we drew up a profile on the board of what each island is like to aid with mapping the key features. The children then chose one of the islands to draw a map of on their A3 grid. The criteria for their maps were as follows:

- It must contain at least four of the landmarks that appeared in the slideshow.

- It must contain a key that demonstrates the scale of the map and any symbols that have been used.

- It must contain at least two settlements.

- It must show at least one transport system (e.g. a road network, train line, canal network).

- It must contain a 100 word description of the island's characteristics and points of interest.

- It must be accompanied by at least five questions about the island for your friends to solve.

Creating the maps takes time but it is well worth it. Just as important as the maps themselves are the questions that the children write to accompany their map. The types of questions that you get will depend on how far the children have progressed in their geometry skills, but they can range from the simple, "What are the coordinates of the Giant Pineapple statue?" to "Which bearing would you need to travel on to reach the town clock from Euclid's farmhouse?" to "If you translated Cashington Towers four spaces to the east and two spaces south, what would be the new set of coordinates?" Try to encourage the pupils to consider the difficulty level of the questions, and ensure there are questions requiring the reader to locate a position or direction of a static object, as well as harder questions that require them to move from one object to another or to translate the position of an object.

With a full complement of maps and accompanying questions, each of them unique in their own way, but with common themes, you have what is nigh on the 'ultimate' differentiated, engaging activity: children spend time going through each other's maps and answering the questions that have been set.

This work also makes for an incredible display item, which, if strategically placed in an area of the school with plenty of traffic, will have people stopping and solving the questions in no time whatsoever. Perfect.

ART

And since geometry is the right foundation of all painting, I have decided to teach its rudiments and principles to all youngsters eager for art.

Albrecht Dürer

I've already mentioned that as a child I didn't view art at school in the most positive light, although for many children it is among their favourite subjects. Not only that, but no exploration of geometry would be complete without at least a brief foray into it. One of the first times that I can genuinely say that I have been blown away by the sheer artistic beauty of something was when I visited the Ali Ben Youssef Madrasa in Marrakech. Although unassuming on the outside, this building opens out into the most magnificent courtyard with walls covered in intricately patterned tiles where shapes seem to drift serenely into each other. The patterns that feature predominately in Islamic art are some of the most creative and visually engaging uses of shape that the world has ever witnessed and can be applied effectively in the primary classroom.

Starting with the image below, I ask the children to tell me everything they can about this picture:

Following this, the children discuss what they have noticed with a partner before being asked a series of questions:

- How many different shapes can you identify?

- Which shape appears most often?

- Are there any shapes that you do not recognise or cannot name?

- How many lines of symmetry are there?

- Why do you think these patterns are so detailed?

Following these questions, we compare and contrast several different images featuring examples of Islamic art, using the above questions to frame our discussion. We particularly focus on the different lines of symmetry present in Islamic designs, as almost all patterns have a vertical line of symmetry in them and many have several lines. This can be a nice stand-alone introductory or even plenary activity when looking at shape or symmetry, but there is a range of ideas you can use on the National Centre for Excellence in the Teaching of Mathematics website[17] – the activity of creating an eight-pointed star from two overlapping squares is a particularly good suggestion.

Another art form that is rich in both culture and scope for application to the teaching of geometry is the mandala. An integral aspect of both Hinduism and Buddhism, mandalas are geometric patterns created as an act of worship. They contain no pictures, only patterns, and are generally symmetrical in both shape and design. The real beauty in certain mandalas comes from the way they are constructed: Tibetan monks create them by carefully funnelling coloured sand into the desired pattern. As you can imagine, this takes a huge amount of time, focus and teamwork, but the finished result is a geometrical masterpiece. You can create mandalas in your classroom with ease using a mandala creator, such as the brilliant ColorMandala application for Google Chrome, which allows you to design your own mandala or select from a range of templates. The programme also allows you to colour in the mandala using a symmetrical paint tool. However, I feel that colouring them in on the computer is too easy, too straightforward and does not reflect the hard work that goes into creating the real thing. I get the children to design the shape of their mandala using ColorMandala, but then we print it out, label the different sections in a paint-by-numbers style, and then get the children to colour it in symmetrically using coloured sand from a craft shop and a piece of paper folded like a funnel. This is very difficult, indeed, but

---

17   See https://www.ncetm.org.uk/resources/18030.

entirely possible with focus; the finished results are far more impressive than a piece of paper churned out from a colour printer.

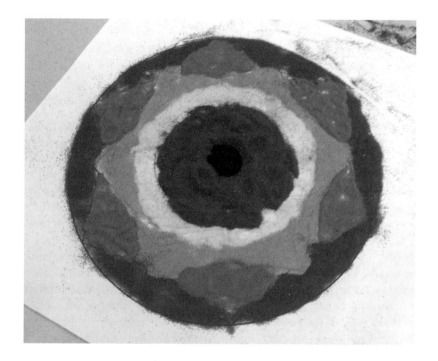

When it comes to specific artists who have wondrous things, geometrically speaking, to teach children, the two names that spring to mind are Piet Mondrian and M. C. Escher.

For when I construct lines and colour combinations on a flat surface, it is with the aim of portraying *universal beauty* as consciously as possible. Nature (or that which I see) inspires me, provides me

– as it does every painter – with the emotion by which I am moved to create something, but I want to approach the truth as closely as possible, abstracting everything until I come to the foundation – still only an outward foundation! – of things. ... I believe that it is possible by means of horizontal and vertical lines, constructed *consciously* but not *calculatingly*, guided by a higher intuition and brought to harmony and rhythm – I believe that these fundamental esthetic shapes – where necessary supplemented by lines in other directions or curved lines, make it possible to arrive at a work of art which is as strong as it is true.[18]

Neoplasticism was Mondrian's attempt to reduce art to a simpler and clearer form, and his most famous pieces of work contain nothing but rectangles of differing sizes in red, yellow and blue, framed by black horizontal and vertical lines on a white background. He certainly achieved his aim of simplicity as primary pupils can work in a neoplastic style without too much hassle. All that is required is white A4 paper, rulers and black, red, yellow and blue felt-tip pens.

- Start by asking the children to draw five lines from top to bottom using a black felt-tip and ruler. Ask them to space out their lines so that the gaps between each line vary. (This is a good point to introduce the children to what 'parallel' means, as each of the black lines should be parallel to the other black lines, providing they have been drawn straight.)

- Next, ask the pupils to draw ten straight lines horizontally across the paper. Explain that each of these lines will be perpendicular to the vertical lines, because at the point where any two lines meet there should be a rectangle. What they should be left with is a grid containing a variety of rectangles of different proportions.

---

18 Letter from Piet Mondrian to the Dutch art critic, Henk Bremmer, 29 January 1914; as quoted in Carel Blotkamp, *Mondrian: The Art of Destruction* (London: Reaktion Books, 2001), p. 81.

- Ask the children to colour in several of the rectangles using the blue, red and yellow felt-tip pens, but to ensure that any rectangle is only coloured in using one colour.

With your newly created pieces of art, the children can investigate all manner of things, from the measurements of the different rectangles to finding out which rectangles are congruent with each other.

Escher's most famous work centres around the art of tessellation. Tessellation is where a shape fits together without any gaps or overlapping. From the tiles in your bathroom to the neat way that a bee creates hexagonal chambers in a honeycomb, shapes that tessellate can be very useful, but not all shapes do tessellate. To investigate this, ask some of the children to draw a three-sided shape, some a four-sided shape, some a five-sided shape, some a six sided-shape, some a seven-sided shape and some an eight-sided shape on A4 paper using a pencil and ruler. At the end of the lesson, collect in the shapes that have been drawn and photocopy each one ten times. In the next lesson, each child gets back their set of shapes and cuts them out carefully. Once cut out, the children can try to fit their tiles together without leaving any gaps. Some will tessellate and some will not. In fact only triangles, quadrilaterals and hexagons tessellate, which makes Escher's work all the more impressive.

Escher doesn't just settle for triangles, quadrilaterals and hexagons either. He incorporates lizards, birds, fish and even Pegasus in his tessellations. Having spent the previous lesson struggling to get simple shapes to fit together, the children are often awestruck by Escher's work: "How many sides does a lizard have?!" And all Escher's designs start from either a triangle, quadrilateral or hexagon, which is then modified by translating part of it to an adjacent side. Admittedly, this is still quite a complicated process but there are some superb interactive tessellation activities online.[19] These enable children to

---

19   See http://www.shodor.org/interactivate/activities/Tessellate/.

modify either a triangle, quadrilateral or hexagon and then click a button to tessellate it.

Hopefully, it is now easier for you to see why maths is beautiful. Without geometry life would be less shapely. In fact, you could even say that it would be pointless …

Chapter 4
MEASUREMENT

I must be at least 500 popcorns tall.

Tim Hopgood

How many popcorns tall are you? For the record, I am roughly 125. Measurement is ace: it's mathematics at its most practical, its most useful. Whether it is working out how many minutes are left of the lesson, how far away something is, or which envelope is bigger, being able to measure things enables us to do all sorts of things in our everyday lives. Despite the significant role it plays in our day-to-day lives, and the scope it offers for enjoyable mathematical activities, measurement is sometimes marginalised in favour of more work on the four operations. So work on measurement inevitably ends up as being a token, half-hearted glance at the basics: making sure that children know how to use a ruler, making sure they can name some of the metric units of measurement and make conversions between them, and making sure they can work out the area and perimeter of some shapes. It does not have to be marginalised though; these important concepts are just as relevant to real life as acres of number crunching.

Children like measurement. It gives them the rare opportunity of getting down to some hands-on maths. The breadth of topics to cover within measurement is huge, so in this chapter we'll just take a look at a few fun activities that you could use to cover the main areas.

Measure what is measurable, and make measurable what is not so.

Galileo

In order to measure something we have to know what unit we are measuring it in. For a stunning start to work on measurement, I tend to begin by reading my class the wonderful story *Big!* by Tim Hopgood.[1] In it, a small boy compares how big he is against all manner of things – skyscrapers, bears, all that jazz – and the highlight is when the little boy tries to approximate his height in terms of popcorn. I stop when I get to this bit in the story, because it's the perfect point for children to get involved in measuring things themselves. The children are given bags of popcorn, cotton wool balls, rolls of kitchen paper, paperclips, shoe laces and whatever else you can lay your hands on in sufficient quantities to make it a practically possible activity. Before the children actually do any real measuring, they must estimate how tall they think they are going to be in their chosen unit of measurement: for example, 50 cotton wool balls tall. Once they have recorded their estimates, they move on to the actual measuring aspect of it. It's not easy trying to measure how tall you are in popcorn or cotton wool, or to convert how tall you are in paper clips into shoelaces. So, this activity is not only loads of fun, but it also serves as a perfect start to learning the following points:

- In order to say how big something is you have to use a unit of measurement. Therefore, it is vitally important that we write down the unit we have measured things in.

- Not all units of measurement are the same. Again, it becomes obvious how important it is that we write down the unit we have measured things in.

The activity also gives the pupils a chance to work on their estimations, which is a vital skill, as estimation provides you with a benchmark to check

---

1   Tim Hopgood, *Big!* (London: Picture Corgi, 2013).

your actual measurement against. You can estimate all kinds of things without leaving the classroom: the height of the room, the circumference of a pupil's head, the mass of a shoe, the capacity of a pencil case. However, for something different, my classes often estimate the size of a variety of animals ... In order to do this, you need to get hold of a copy of *Actual Size* by Steve Jenkins.[2] This picture book illustrates different animals and their body parts. But, and here's the twist, the pictures themselves are life size, so we get to see exactly how long a giant anteater's tongue is,[3] as well as how small a pygmy mouse lemur's hand is compared to a gorilla's. The best way to use this book is in tandem with a slideshow. Project an image of one of the animals in the book on the board, and ask the children to estimate the size of either the animal or of a specific body part. Then, once they have made an estimation, show them the actual size. Once you have done one animal, you can ask the pupils not only to estimate the size of the next animal, but also to compare it to the size of the previous animal.

Another super way of approaching estimating measurements is through examining the imaginary belongings of a giant. Trisha Lee, of Make Believe Arts,[4] uses the story of the Empress of Lilliput finding giant footprints and then a giant as a context for exploring proportion, measuring and scale.[5] I have my own twist on this idea. It begins with the children entering the classroom to find a giant leaf (cut out of either green card or paper) in the middle of the floor with the question, "Where has this leaf come from?" written across it. We discuss the potential origins of the leaf, and I guide the conversation towards the fact that it is, in fact, a truly giant leaf, much bigger than anything that we have ever seen before. We then turn over the

---

2   Steve Jenkins, *Actual Size* (New York: Harcourt Brace and Co., 2011).

3   60 cm.

4   See http://www.makebelievearts.co.uk/.

5   See http://static.squarespace.com/static/53ad7934e4b0a25fee7c47b2/t/53e0bb5ce4b0a86 a2dc05e26/1407236956797/Mathematics%20Programs.pdf.

leaf to find a copy of *Jim and the Beanstalk* by Raymond Briggs underneath.[6] (This story is set in the aftermath of Jack's adventure up the beanstalk. But, in this case, the giant Jim encountered was far from fierce and struggling with the reality of growing old: the giant was going bald, losing his eyesight and his teeth were falling out. Jim, being a good spirited chap, offers to help the giant by measuring him so he can get a pair of glasses, some false teeth and a wig.) Following the story, I ask the children, "What other items do you think the giant might like, and how big do you think they would need to be?" After some discussion, I pull out a giant's toothbrush from behind my desk, which is actually a plastic broom with its head pulled off and stuck back on so that it lays along the length of the handle. We compare this toothbrush to a normal toothbrush, and the children estimate how many times bigger it is. We then measure both the normal toothbrush and the giant one. Using the giant toothbrush as a guide, the children then have to estimate exactly how big the giant versions of some of the other items they suggested would be: for example, how big would a giant spoon have to be? What about a giant pencil? It needn't be just estimating length or size: the children could estimate the mass of a giant's shoe by measuring the weight of their own shoe (with scales); they could estimate the volume of liquid a giant's mug might hold, or estimate the surface area of a giant's table.

So, a useful maxim to remember: estimation before measurement.

---

6   Raymond Briggs, *Jim and the Beanstalk* (New York: PaperStar, 1970).

LENGTH

Length manifests itself in many different forms: height, width, depth, distance and even perimeter, and so measuring length is never merely concerned with length alone. Not only that, but we use the word 'length' when talking about measuring time (such as the 'length' of a film or how 'long' it has been between events). The length that we are talking about here is anything that can be measured using millimetres, centimetres, metres, kilometres or inches, feet, miles.

So, where to start with length? Well, having got the children to measure themselves using popcorn it will have become obvious to them that there must be a better tool for measuring length. There is. A ruler. Despite it being a remarkably simple tool, there is one thing kids need to know about rulers straightaway, and that is to start measuring from 0. Children do not automatically measure from 0 because they are used to counting from 1, and so they start measuring from the 1 cm mark. Once your pupils know how to measure using a ruler, you can introduce them to other tools for measuring length – such as tape measures and trundle wheels – and start discussing which tools you would use for measuring different things. Why, for example, would you use a tape measure to measure the distance from the floor to the ceiling? (Because the ruler isn't long enough.)

Once the children know the tools of the trade, you can put some creativity into deciding what they are going to measure. The age old approach is to get them to measure whatever they can lay their hands on in the classroom, and there is nothing wrong with this, as it provides a good starting point for practising converting units of measurement (e.g. millimetres into centimetres), which is a vital skill. However, there are only so many times that a child can measure the length of a pencil and remain enthused. Paper aeroplanes are a far more exciting thing altogether, and are a guaranteed win in terms of children's enthusiasm. *The Great Paper Caper* by Oliver Jeffers[7] tells the tale of a bear desperate to win the 112th Biennial Paper Airplane competition, and it's a great context to play within when working on measuring lengths. The children can measure the dimensions of the paper aeroplane as they build it using a ruler, but the best bit is measuring the distance they can fly! Unless the flight is deeply unsuccessful, the pupils will get to use tape measures and trundle wheels for this bit. There are added benefits to this activity: you can use it as a context for working on data handling by presenting the results of the competition in a chart or graph, as well as using the results for working out the differences in distance flown by the different competitors.

If you don't fancy paper aeroplanes, measuring mazes can be great fun. Start by telling the children that their challenge for today is to create a maze for ants. Provide them with a pile of craft matchsticks,[8] a sheet of card, a sticky note and a pot of PVA glue. Ask the children to stick the matchsticks onto the card to create a maze. The walls of the maze must be wide enough to fit a ruler between them, and must be complex enough to pose an ant a problem, while still being simple enough to measure. Once the children have created their maze, they should measure their route through the maze in straight lines, using a ruler. Ask them to write down their measurements on the sticky note before swapping their maze with a partner, who should check their measurements for accuracy by measuring the route again. This maze idea can be extended further by telling the tale of Theseus and the Minotaur, then getting the children to construct large mazes using sports cones or desks flipped on to their sides to create the walls. As this maze is much bigger than the one we made for ants, you have to explain that it's no longer appropriate to use a ruler to measure the length of the route. Remind the pupils that Theseus unravelled a ball of string to mark out his route through the Minotaur's maze, and ask how they could use string to measure the length of the route through their own maze. By collecting up the string

---

7   Oliver Jeffers, *The Great Paper Caper* (London: HarperCollins Children's Books, 2009).
8   Normal matchsticks but with the end cut off so they cannot be struck.

at the end, the pupils can measure the string against a tape measure (or by repeatedly measuring ruler lengths). A good question to ask at the end of this activity is whether the pupils think that using a piece of string is an accurate way of measuring, thereby opening up a discussion about accuracy and margins of error.

Before we move on to area, a quick word on perimeter. I have worked with lots of children who are confused by the concept of perimeter purely because they make it more complicated than it needs to be. Perimeter is the same as length; it is just the length around the outside of an object. If you can measure length and carry out simple addition then perimeter should be easy. Area on the other hand can be a little bit more tricky ...

AREA

Area is a measure of the size of a surface. It is a two-dimensional measurement and is measured in a unit of length that is squared – for example, mm^2 or cm^2 or m^2. You can have surfaces that are different shapes but still cover the same surface area:

1	2	3	4	5	6	7	8	9

1	2	3
4	5	6
7	8	9

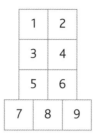

Learning about area generally begins with shapes made out of squared paper. The children then count the number of squares present within the shape to find the area:

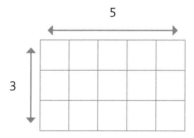

This then progresses on to shapes that are on squared paper but contain half-squares, like this triangle:

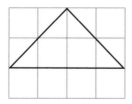

Eventually, the helpful squares are removed and calculating the area becomes more tricky. However, it is only a little more tricky because all we really need to remember are two formulae:

1   The area of a rectangle is worked out by multiplying the length by the width:

area = length x width

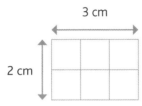

3 cm x 2 cm = 6 cm²

2   The area of a triangle is worked out by multiplying half by the base times the perpendicular height:

area = ½ x base x perpendicular height

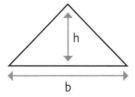

$^1/_2$ x 3 cm x 2 cm = 3 cm²

The reason why you only really need to know these two formulae is because you can generally work out the area of other shapes by breaking them into rectangles or triangles:[9]

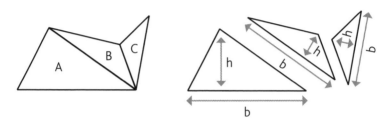

One of the most common activities for investigating area is measuring the school playground. This can be a great activity, but for a bit more variety I like to ask the children to work out the area of different classrooms in the school by measuring them. Following on from this there is a great piece of work that can be linked with our work on geometry. Remember the project that I talked about to design a new school building in the chapter on geometry? Well, that dealt with the exterior design of the building, but what if we wanted to look at the interior as well? Planner 5D is an application that lets you create 2D floor plans and then allows you to explore them in 3D.[10] The great thing about this application is that you can set the dimensions of each room, so it provides the perfect context for exploring the area of rooms. Pupils can work with the dimensions either displayed or hidden, in metric or imperial and, because of how easy it is to adapt the layout of the floor plan, they can explore what happens to the area of the room when they change the length, width or overall shape.

---

9   Except the circle, but you've already got the formula for that one.
10   See https://planner5d.com/.

VOLUME AND CAPACITY

Volume and capacity: the terms are often used interchangeably but mean different things. Volume is the measure of space taken up by something and is generally measured in m³ or similar. Capacity is the measure of how much something can hold and is generally measured in litres. Volume is concerned not just with length and width, but also height. For example, to work out the volume of a cuboid you multiply the length by the width by the height:

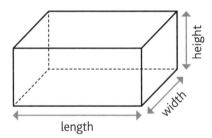

Measuring the volume of shapes in the primary classroom, however, is best carried out not through formulae but through practical activities and, for me, the best resources for working with volume are cubed centimetre blocks or Cuisenaire rods. A good way to start is to create a cuboid by stacking cubes on top of one another and asking the children to count the cubes to work out the volume of the shape. Repeat this with lots of different sized cuboids until the children are confident. Once they have grasped counting cubes, I like to move on to approximating the volume of different containers by stacking the centimetre cubes inside. This can be difficult with some containers, particularly circular ones like cups, but it is yet another exercise in estimation and approximation. Food packaging works particularly well, as not only does it come in a wide range of shapes and sizes, but it also has the benefit that it can be deconstructed into a net. This allows the pupils to measure the surface area of the different parts of the packaging, and it provides a great context for beginning to explore the relationship between surface area and volume.

Capacity is best explored by investigating the amount of liquid different containers can hold. A nice way of doing this is by giving groups of pupils five empty plastic containers and asking them to place them in order of how much liquid they will hold. The children will often assume that the tallest container will hold the most liquid, but will not necessarily take into account the width of the container. Children are often surprised that a shorter and wider container can hold more liquid. Once you have got them ordering different containers, you can use capacity as a great opportunity to work on their estimation skills. Grab ten or more different containers, the more varied the better, and fill the first container with liquid. The children then note down the capacity of the first container in their books. Next, they are shown container number two and are asked to predict the capacity of it, using the first container as a benchmark. We then fill the second container and I give the children an acceptable margin of error for the prediction e.g. 50 ml, and if they correctly estimate the amount the container will hold they get a point. Repeat this with as many containers as you have to hand. This activity can be shaken up a bit by sharing the capacity of the first container with the pupils but then asking them to estimate the remaining containers all at once, without going through each container in turn. You can also add in more unlikely containers such as shoes, resealable bags and plastic gloves. You cannot underestimate the value of activities that practise estimation.

MASS

First things first: mass is not the same thing as weight. Mass is a measure of how much matter something has, whereas weight is a measure of the force pulling us downwards – that is, gravity. When we talk about grams and kilograms, we are actually talking about mass not weight. It goes without saying that some of the best activities to do with investigating mass require nothing more than scales and some objects to measure. However, if you want to try a different activity, the following one works like a dream. It is a rehash of one of Brucey's family TV game shows, in which the children have to guess 'higher or lower' or, in this case, 'more or less'. I set up a table at the front of the room with five identical mixing bowls placed on it and some kitchen scales. In each of the mixing bowls is a different object. All the children need is a piece of paper with a large arrow drawn on one side and space to record the results on the other. I weigh the first object and ask a volunteer to read the mass off the scales, then call out the answer to the rest of the class. I then show the pupils what the next item is and ask them to predict whether it will weigh more or less by turning their arrow to point upwards if they think it will weigh more and downwards if they think it will weigh less. We then weigh the item and repeat the process. This game can be scaled up in difficulty by asking pupils to predict not only whether something weighs more or less, but to predict the actual mass of each object, with the pupils aiming to get within 100 grams of the correct answer.

There is a slight twist on this game, which can be used to reinforce the point that not all objects have the same mass even if they have the same volume. Using the same format as above, I replace the mixing bowls with plastic beakers, which are filled to the same point with five different substances. Although there is the same amount of each different substance, the mass will vary between each beaker depending on the density of the substance.

TIME

What a measure to finish on! Ask any primary teacher to list the area of maths that most frequently stumps their pupils and telling the time on an analogue clock would be pretty high up the list. The usefulness of being able to tell the time on an analogue clock is debatable nowadays, particularly with the proliferation of digital gadgets that, as adults, we rarely leave home without, all of which contain a digital clock. However, the fact remains that not being able to tell the time on an analogue clock makes you look daft, so spare your children the blushes and do your best to get them reading the time with confidence.

So, what are the areas where children tend to trip up on when telling the time?

1   The hour hand and the minute hand: which is which? Remembering which hand points to the minutes and which points to the hours can cause difficulty. I've heard of a few different ways to remember this, but still feel that repeatedly reinforcing that the big hand points to the minutes and the short hand points to the hours works best. Just keep going over it again and again.

2   How many minutes is that? There is no point in teaching time unless children understand their 5 times table. The children's attention must be drawn to the small lines around the edge of the clock face that represent one minute and that there are five small gaps between each large number on the clock face, meaning that each large number represents five minutes. The children should be taught to count in fives going clockwise around the face until they are near the minute hand and then to count in ones from there.

3   Why is the hour hand not pointing at an hour? As each hour progresses, the minute hand moves visibly around the clock face in a

clockwise fashion, but so does the hour hand. It is vital that, even from an early stage in a child's learning of time, they use clocks that demonstrate this hour hand movement correctly. Clocks that allow free manipulation of the hands, although convenient, can cause misconceptions when used by pupils as the minute hand can be moved without the hour hand, not to mention that the hands can be rotated anti-clockwise. Try to use geared clocks wherever possible, as these simulate how the hour hand moves round over the course of an hour.

4   Is it 'past' or 'to'? The terminology associated with writing or saying the time as a sentence can also prove problematic, because any time before the half-past mark is referred to as minutes 'past' the current hour and any time after the half-past mark is referred to as minutes 'to' the next hour. In order to support pupils with their work on saying the time after the half-past mark, ensure that they practise subtracting from 60 as this will enable them to work out how many minutes 'to' more efficiently. For further reinforcement, you can also shade in the side of the clock face that deals with minutes 'past' in one colour and minutes 'to' in another colour.

5   The 24-hour clock. This one is just a case of reminding the pupils to apply a bit of mental arithmetic. If the hour is after midday then whatever hour it is they should add 12 to it to get the 24 hour time (e.g. 4 p.m. + 12 = 16:00).

In terms of learning the basics of how to tell the time, I truly believe that the more traditional approaches of spending plenty of time practising using clocks to read and replicate time is the best approach. To supplement this, I have used a wonderful programme from Nessy Learning over the last couple of years called Clock Island.[11] This programme is personalised to each child, records their progress and uses regular check-ups to see what is still causing

11   See http://www.nessy.com/uk/.

them difficulties. As a diagnostic tool it is brilliant, but, more importantly, the kids just love playing the games!

What I really like about teaching time is looking at the measurement itself. We are taught that there are 60 seconds in a minute, 60 minutes in an hour and 24 hours in a day, but have you ever considered that there is more to time than seconds, minutes, hours and days? How about how far a humpback whale's song travels in one second?[12] Or how many barrels of oil are used around the world in one minute?[13] Or by how much does the population of India increase in one day?[14]

Just a Second by Steve Jenkins sells itself as "a different way to look at time", and it most certainly is.[15] The book not only gives you neat comparisons of what happens in a given unit of time, it also explains how we have come to use the units for measuring time that we do. Pupils can use this to create their own way of looking at time by coming up with things that are personal to their life that happen in one second, one minute, one hour, one day, one week, one month and one year.

I also love looking at time zones, and still find it fascinating that, as I sit here typing while munching on my cereal, somewhere else in the world people are just getting ready for bed. An old favourite of mine is *All in a Day* by Mitsumasa Anno and friends.[16] It tells the story of nine different children's experiences of New Year in different time zones around the world, with each child's story drawn by a different illustrator. However, even this book, which is absolute class, has recently been trumped by one of the most beautifully illustrated and well thought out books I have ever had the pleasure

---

12   1550 m.
13   59,000 barrels.
14   47,000 people.
15   Steve Jenkins, *Just a Second* (New York: Houghton Mifflin Harcourt, 2011).
16   Mitsumasa Anno, *All in a Day* (New York: Puffin Books, 1999).

of delving into: *At the Same Moment Around the World* by Clotilde Perrin.[17] As you open the first page you are transported to 6 a.m. in Dakar, Senegal, where Keita is helping his father pull in the morning catch. As you turn the page again, you find yourself with Benedict drinking hot chocolate at 7 a.m. in Paris. Each page moves on eastwards to another place in a country that is one hour further ahead, and on to another child going about their daily life. From Sofia to Baghdad, Dubai to Samarkand, the Himalayas to Hanoi, Shanghai to Tokyo, Ayers Rock to Noumea, Anadyr to Apia, Honolulu to Anchorage, San Francisco to Phoenix, Mexico City to Lima, Manaus to Nuuk, Fernando de Noronha to a cruise ship in the middle of the Atlantic, before finishing up back where we started in Dakar. Everything that occurs in this book happens at the same moment. When you read this to the kids they become ever more excited, and you are given the gift of a room full of little eyes becoming wider and brighter as you progress through the book.

---

17 Clotilde Perrin, *At the Same Moment Around the World* (San Francisco, CA: Chronicle, 2014).

Chapter 5
STATISTICS

Statistical thinking will one day be as necessary for efficient citizenship as the ability to read and write.

Samuel S. Wilks[1]

In an increasingly data driven society, the need for some form of grounding in statistical thinking has become increasingly important. Yet, despite this, statistics forms a relatively small part of the primary mathematics curriculum. Small it may well be, but please don't make statistics an afterthought in your curriculum planning, as it deserves proper attention.

The fact is that, despite its mathematical base, statistics is as much an art as it is a science.

Darrell Huff[2]

Have you ever looked at a statistic and thought, surely that can't be true? For me, the most recent occasion when I found myself thinking exactly this was when I read an article on the BBC news website about the TV coverage benefits for the sponsors of the Tour de France.[3] In the article, Cyril Du Cluzeau, marketing manager for French sports brand Le Coq Sportif, is quoted as saying that four billion people will watch the cycling event in

---

1   Samuel S. Wilks, presidential address to the American Statistical Association, *Journal of the Acoustical Society of America* 46(253) (1951): 1–18.
2   Darrell Huff, *How to Lie With Statistics* (New York: W.W. Norton, 1993).
3   See http://www.bbc.co.uk/news/business-22854929.

2014. I found myself thinking that seemed awfully high. Over half of the world's population are going to watch a loads of blokes pedalling around France? Surely not. A couple of weeks later, this article appeared as the topic of an article in the Small Data section of the BBC's Magazine Monitor.[4]

Anthony Reuben does a fine job of sniffing out unusual and often spurious data that has appeared in recent news articles. In the case of the four billion supposed viewers of the Tour de France, Reuben shows just how much uncertainty there can be surrounding the use of statistics and the methods used to work them out. He is unable to get to the bottom of where the four billion figure came from, but is equally shocked by the figure of 3.5 billion people who apparently watched the Tour de France in 2013. In that year, the BBC said that 6.5 million people watched the tour over the three weeks that it was on. In 2013, Chris Froome, a Brit, won the tour and yet BBC figures show that only about 10% of the British population watched it.

Reuben also references the viewing figures by KantarSport on the FIFA 2010 World Cup,[5] where the global audience was worked out by taking the viewing figures of 17 countries and extrapolating from there. This only gave a figure of 2.2 billion people who watched for at least 20 consecutive minutes, or 3.2 billion people who watched for at least a minute. Reuben highlights that for both the FIFA World Cup and the Tour de France, one of the key restricting factors for viewing figures was the number of people watching in China, India, the USA and Russia because of the sheer size of the population in these countries. He therefore concludes that unless bicycle racing is extremely popular in these crucial markets, it is very unlikely that the suggested viewing figures for either the 2013 or 2014 Tour de France are accurate.

---

4   See http://www.bbc.co.uk/news/blogs-magazine-monitor-28264183.
5   See http://www.fifa.com/mm/document/affederation/tv/01/47/32/73/2010fifaworldcupsou thafricatvaudiencereport.pdf.

So, why is it important that our children learn how to spot when some marketing rogue from a French sports brand is playing fast and loose with the numbers? Well, you could well argue that it isn't, but the simple fact is that when 45.6% of all statistics are made up, interpreting information is key to being a well-rounded human. Whether it is social cues, spoken and written language or data, critical interpretation allows for more effective decision making.

DATA

What is data?

a A collection of facts and figures.

b The name of a character from *Star Trek* with questionable make-up.[6]

c A good name for a pet gerbil.

Well, it can't be answer (b) because 'data' was written without a capital letter, and it can't be (c) because everyone knows that you should always call a pet gerbil Gerry, so I guess the answer is (a). At its most simple, data is a collection of facts and figures, but the truth is that data can be anything but simple. Data can be qualitative (descriptive) (e.g. maths is the most important subject in primary school) or quantitative (numerical) (e.g. 29% of reception children would like to be a dinosaur when they grow up). When studying primary mathematics, we tend to focus on quantitative data and this can come in two flavours: discrete and continuous.

---

6 Should have gone to Specsavers?

Discrete data[7] can only be of a certain value and cannot be split into a smaller unit (e.g. the number of PE socks Anne has lost this term, because Anne cannot lose half a sock, only whole socks). As discrete data has a finite set of values, it is often counted rather than measured. Continuous data, on the other hand, is measured – it can be of any value within a given range (e.g. the length of Leo's pet stick insect, Twig, can be of any length within the range of however long stick insects grow).

So, now we know what data is, how do we get our hands on it?

COLLECTING DATA

Knock knock.

Teacher: Come in.

Gabby: Excuse me, Miss, but can we ask your class a few questions?

Teacher: Well, we're right in the middle of something, girls. Can it wait until after break?

Michelle: Not really, Miss. Sir says we need to have this done and be back in class in less than five minutes.

Teacher: OK, girls, what do you need to ask us?

Michelle: About your favourite crisps.

Gabby: Right, hands up if you like cheese and onion.

---

7   See http://www.mathsisfun.com/data/data.html

Surveys are perhaps the easiest way to collect data. No doubt, at some point in your teaching career, you will have heard the nervous knock on your classroom door of pupils from another class who have been sent your way to carry out a survey. Generally, these exercises seek to survey your class's favourite crisps/sweets/pets/TV programme/pop star/football player/colour. I have nothing against this, as it is important that children are given the opportunity to carry out surveys, but there are a few rules it helps to follow:

- Arrange a suitable time with the other class teacher beforehand rather than sending the children along unannounced. That way the other class won't be too annoyed when their very interesting and important lesson on rivers is interrupted. This also has the added benefit of reducing the likelihood of Mike using his survey time to have a water fight in the boys' toilets as not only do you know where he should be, but so does the other teacher. Make sure that you remind Mike of this before he sets off.

- Train your class in how to conduct their survey by ensuring that they know the importance of giving their participants all of the options before asking them to select their preference. Also, make sure they realise that being unwaveringly polite to the other class teacher is not up for debate and that thanking them, and their class, for their time and participation is vital.

- The most important rule is to make sure that it matters. We want children to realise that statistical analysis can give us vital informa-tion, which can be incredibly useful. Unless you are setting up a school tuck shop or petting zoo, knowing about the children's preferences for cheese and onion crisps and guinea pigs is not particularly useful.

So, how can we make their surveys matter? I have said this already but children like to be valued, particularly for the work they have produced. To see the look of pride on a 7-year-old's face when they get that gold star for getting all of their tables correct is a simple pleasure from which even the most battle-hardened of veterans still derives a warm feeling. However, we also know that the shiny feeling of a gold star is temporary and, unless more gold stars are awarded, the lustre starts to fade. For a longer lasting shine, the children need opportunities for their work to be part of something more than just a quest for a further gold star. So, why not use your statistics work as a way of engaging pupils in some genuine school research?

I once had a class who were as eager as I was to improve the attitude towards maths in our school. They were delightfully positive little souls who seemingly enjoyed anything you would throw at them, particularly if it was mathematical. They could not understand why they heard other kids in the school speaking disparagingly about maths as, for many of them, it was their favourite subject. This was the impetus for a superb survey on the school's attitude towards mathematics. It was decided that the pupils would work in pairs to come up with one question they would investigate by surveying the rest of the school. This would give us a set of questions that would hopefully paint a picture of how the pupils perceived mathematics.

So, our objective was to find out how pupils at the school felt about mathematics. We decided to carry out a census (the whole pupil community) rather than a sample (a small group of pupils selected randomly) because, although it could take more time to administer, it would give us more dependable results. The next step was to design our questionnaire. In order to do this, pupils were asked to write ten questions that would help them to find out what their peers thought about maths. We looked at the differences between open and closed questions and how they would impact on carrying out the survey and presenting our findings. We decided that our survey would comprise mostly of closed questions, as these would be quicker to administer in the classroom and would allow us to show our results more easily in graphs.

Some of the questions that were put forward as suggestions for our census included:

- Do you hate maths?

- What is your favourite area of mathematics (selecting from number and calculations, shape and geometry, measurement and data handling)?

- Are times tables easy or hard?

- Would you like there to be more or less maths during the school week?

- Do you do any extra maths at home?

- What is your favourite maths website?

- Do you ever do maths activities for fun?

- Do you prefer times tables or reading?

- Maths is the best subject – do you agree?

- Who is your favourite teacher?

- What do you find most difficult during maths lessons?

- How would you rank maths in terms of enjoyment? (1: I hate it to 5: I love it)

- How long do you usually spend on maths homework per week?

- Do your parents like maths?

- What topic would you like to go over again in maths?

- What is your favourite maths resource?

- Who would win: a penguin or three squirrels?[8]

- Would you like to study maths when you are older?

- Do you think that maths is important?

- Is maths valued at this school?

- Do you use maths when you are not at school?

- What is the most important thing that helps you to learn maths?

- Would you like to be better at maths?

- If you could stop learning about maths tomorrow, would you do so?

We then went through all of the questions and picked out those that were as neutral as possible, that did not lead the participants to an answer and that were not too similar to each other (e.g. "Do you use maths when you are not at school?" was considered to be too similar to "Do you do any extra maths at home?"). We ended up with a set of 12 questions which the class then used to survey the school. After the results had been collected and analysed, the findings were presented to the head, who was suitably impressed with their work, followed by the wider school community. This had a far more profound effect on the motivation of my class than any survey about favourite flavours or footballers, because they felt that what they were doing was contributing to the development of the school they loved attending. Your survey need not be about maths, though, it could be about any number of things to do with the school.

Another way that I like to conduct surveys is to ask the children to complete a secret investigation. This is a very simple idea but the kids love it. In their maths lesson, they come up with one question that they want to investigate

---

8   Some needed reminding of our objective ...

throughout the rest of the day. The question must be simple and be something to do with daily school life (e.g. "How many minutes do we spend on writing in each lesson?" or "In which lesson do the most hands go up?"). The child then keeps a little record of this throughout the rest of the day (ensuring that it does not disrupt their other lessons) and uses the data next lesson to create a graph.

However, sometimes you just want to work on presenting and analysing data without having to go through the process of collecting it first. This is where secondary sources come in. Flick through the average maths textbook and you are likely to find various examples of surveys on fictional classes about their favourite crisps, colours, footballers and so on. These can be fine for a quick fix but, once again, they do little to heighten the children's sense of the importance of statistics. There are far more meaningful sets of statistics readily available on all manner of topics.

A source that I love to delve into is the wonderful book, *If the World Were a Village*, by David J. Smith.[9] This looks at the lifestyles of people around the world, covering everything from the religions they practice, to the languages they speak, to the access they have to clean water and food. The truly great thing about it, though, is that it makes the data far easier to interpret by turning the 6.7 billion[10] people of the world[11] into a theoretical global village of just 100 people, meaning that one person in the village represents 67 million people in the real world. The possibilities for using this book as a source of data for drawing graphs are vast, from simple comparisons between the 76 people in the global village who have electricity compared to the 24 that do not, to more detailed comparisons such as the division of money and possessions. The book is certainly not short of points for discussion, and

---

9   David J. Smith, *If the World Were a Village: A Book about the World's People* (Toronto: Kids Can Press, 2008).

10   They interpret billion as one thousand million or 1,000,000,000.

11   The data used in my copy is from 2008.

every time I have used it in the classroom it has provided a great deal more than just some figures for us to put into a bar chart.

A further source of data which is more palatable, interesting and serious than those lurking in a textbook can be found in the form of infographics. An infographic is a way of presenting often complex information in a simplified way through a combination of pictures, diagrams and text. Take a look at the infographic below and think how best you could use the information for creating some charts of your own:

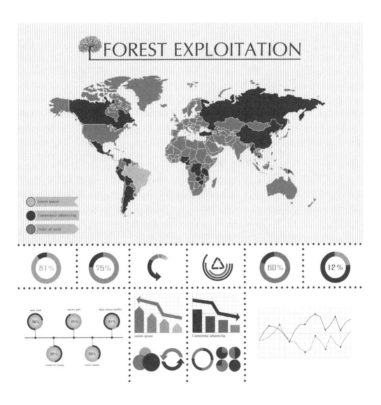

Infographics can be found easily on the internet, with websites such as www.dailyinfographic.com containing vast quantities of different infographics organised by category.[12] There are also some cracking books on infographics. The 'Big Countdown' range is particularly effective at taking a visual stance on stars, the rainforest, the human body, poisonous plants, the animal kingdom and planet earth. The recently published Information Graphics books, *Human Body*[13] and *Animal Kingdom*,[14] researched by Simon Rogers and illustrated by Peter Grundy and Nicholas Blechman, are also worth a look, particularly as any infographic about the finer points of our digestive system (read: poo) is bound to get the kids interested!

You can create your own infographics easily either by drawing them yourself by hand or by using ICT. There are several excellent web services and applications that are specifically designed to help you to create your own infographics, such as Piktochart and Infogram. These apps are surprisingly simple to use and could be used by your class as well as yourself.

So, we've got some data – what should we do with it?

---

12 I like the one on dog world records: http://dailyinfographic.com/dog-world-records-infographic, and the one on deadliest pandemics: http://dailyinfographic.com/wp-content/uploads/2011/12/GOOD-deadliest-pandemics.jpeg, but would suggest that you check the content of all of them first as I would not recommend the rude hand gestures from around the world infographic.

13 Simon Rogers, *Information Graphics: Human Body* (Dorking: Big Picture Press, 2014).

14 Simon Rogers, *Information Graphics: Animal Kingdom* (Dorking: Big Picture Press, 2014).

DRAWING GRAPHS

As we've already covered in the chapter on geometry, graphical skills don't necessarily come easily to everyone. Drawing charts, graphs and tables can, along with drawing shapes, be incredibly challenging for some pupils. However, you can maximise your pupils' chances of success by insisting on them following the golden rules of graphing:

- Always use a ruler and pencil.

- Draw all charts, tables and graphs on squared paper.

- Plot value labels on axes without leaving squares in between (this minimises the likelihood that the children will space out their values unevenly).

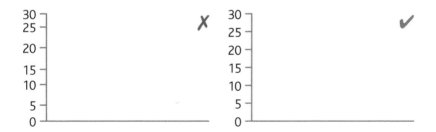

- Always label axes clearly and accurately. If the label is supposed to be on the line, then make sure that it is on the line and not in the next square.

- Use a ruler to line up points to the axes, particularly if the point falls on a value that is between axis labels.

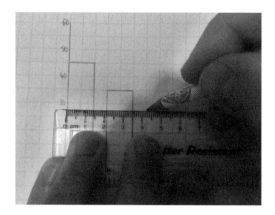

- Get a visualiser.

- Resist the temptation to use Excel. At least most of the time ...

This last point is an important one. Excel and other spreadsheet applications are fantastic tools for creating charts, but they have downsides:

- They do not build the necessary manual graphical skills and confidence.

- The children will be more interested in changing the aesthetics of their chart and less likely to focus on the data.[15]

- It means a dreaded trip to the ICT suite, which you could probably do without on a Monday morning.

There is a time and a place for using Excel to create charts, but just make sure that the children get plenty of opportunities to draw them manually.

---

15 Polka dot background bubble chart, anyone?

Data can also be presented in simple form by putting it in a table. But, other than tables, what charts do the children need to know about?

TALLY CHARTS, PICTOGRAMS AND BLOCK DIAGRAMS

Initially, children should experience presenting data in formats that do not use axes with values on them. Tally charts are simple ways of achieving this. They are not only straightforward ways of presenting data, but are also incredibly useful ways of recording numerical data.

One of my favourite charts of all is the pictogram. These simple graphs use a picture or icon to represent a certain amount or number of things. This type of graph is perfect for comparing relative amounts (e.g. the number of books read by different members of the class over a school year).

Books Read

= 10 books

To begin with, get children used to working with pictograms that have simple values, such as each icon being worth 2 or 10. The benefits of using these values are that they are relatively easy to count in and, when split in half, they give us a whole number. This means we can have pictograms that look like this:

Books Read

📖 = 10 books

The only potential difficulty with creating pictograms is that it can be quite hard to replicate even a simple icon accurately, which means you will often get something like this:

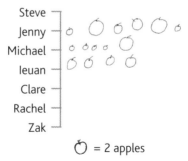

🍎 = 2 apples

A good way to get around this is to find images or clipart on your computer that work well with the topic of your pictogram and repeatedly copy and paste the image to give yourself a sheet of little icons that the children can cut out and stick to form a perfect pictogram. Even better than that, why not use some actual items to create a real life pictogram. Here's one I made about the number of apples eaten:

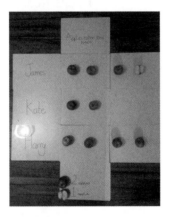

The downside of pictograms is that it can be difficult to show certain values – for example, if an icon equals 10 then it is very difficult to show a value of 11.

So, what do we need for more accuracy?

BAR CHART

The introduction of bar charts sees the use of axes with labels, which allows for more accurate readings and greater flexibility in terms of the data you are plotting. As with pictograms, bar charts are designed to allow you to compare differing amounts – for example, which pet is liked the most:

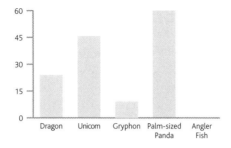

Providing you follow the golden rules listed above, bar charts aren't all that bad, and once the children have got the axes sorted there is little holding them back. One of the things I most like to do with bar charts is to make them massive. This is simple to do and requires little more than something adhesive, a ruler to measure with, a pen to label with, a pair of scissors to snip with and a selection of coloured rolls of Bordette to make the edges of displays look neat and tidy.[16] On a suitable wall, make a pair of axes by sticking two strips of white or black Bordette perpendicular to each other. Then, using the ruler and pen, label your axes, making sure that you space them out evenly. Once you have a pair of labelled axes, you can start adding bars by measuring and cutting out the correct length of a piece of coloured piece of border roll, and sticking it down to create the desired individual bars of your chart.

---

16 Make sure that it is the straight edged stuff and not that awful scalloped edged, corrugated rubbish.

LINE GRAPH

Line graphs are used for a different purpose to the other graphs we've looked at so far. The line graph is designed to show the changes in information that are connected in some way – for example, how the temperature changes over the course of a day or a year.

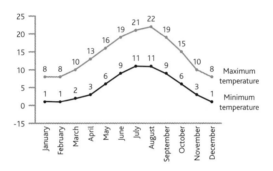

A fun way to get children enthused about line graphs is to create a 'My Moody Day' graph. All you need for this is a pair of axes, with the x axis representing time and the y axis representing the strength of your mood. The premise is simple: tell the children a short story about a day in which you were in a particular mood, such as excited or angry, and they try to show this on their graph by drawing a line that goes either up or down as the events of the day unfold.

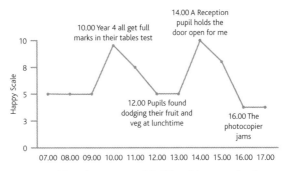

How happy was Mr Tiley-Nunn today?

You can also use this sort of chart in reverse for a literacy task, by giving the children the Moody Day graph and asking them to write what happened during the day.

And now for the most difficult of all graphs …

PIE CHARTS

I find pie charts a bit annoying, to be honest. They are clever little things and make reading comparisons of amounts incredibly easy. So, what's the problem then? Well, if you have ever tried drawing pie charts with young children you will have an understanding of my frustration. They are far from simple to draw, requiring the use of not only a ruler but also a pair of compasses and a protractor. However, the tricky process can be broken down into six (relatively) straightforward steps:

1   Put all of your data into a table and add up the total in the final column:

Frogs	Rabbits	Parrots	Stick insects	Total
6	9	2	3	20

2   Turn the data into percentages by dividing each value by the total and multiplying by 100:

Frogs	Rabbits	Parrots	Stick insects	Total
6 ÷ 20 x 100 = 30%	9 ÷ 20 x 100 = 45%	2 ÷ 20 x 100 = 10%	3 ÷ 20 x 100 = 15%	100%

3   You then have to work out how big each slice of the pie is going to be by turning the percentages into degrees, which will add up to make 360°:

Frogs	Rabbits	Parrots	Stick insects	Total
30 ÷ 100 x 360 = 108°	45 ÷ 100 x 360 = 162°	10 ÷ 100 x 360 = 36°	15 ÷ 100 x 360 = 54°	360°

4   Now that you have your degrees for each sector or pie slice, you need to draw a circle to put your slices into using a pair of compasses.

5   Once you have your circle you can start measuring your sectors using a protractor:

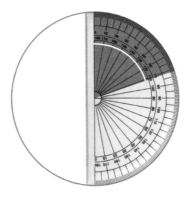

6   Once all of your sectors have been drawn in, you should end up with something that looks like this:

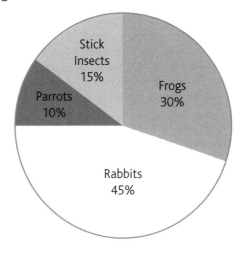

Another way that you can create pie charts is by introducing some clay modelling at step 4. By using a circular pastry cutter, you can create pie charts out of circles of clay. The benefits of these are that, once you have marked out the sectors, you can cut them into pieces and they make pretty awesome exploding 3D pie charts!

VENN DIAGRAMS

Sometimes we don't want to count or measure things, but to group them. What does a scarab beetle have in common with a caribou?[17] How is a slow loris linked to a python?[18] *Zoo-ology* by Joelle Jolivet[19] is a book about grouping animals, but not in a way that we are normally accustomed to. There are no mentions of kingdoms, phyla or genera, because each delectable double-page spread contains illustrations of animals grouped together by one simple characteristic: hot, cold, freshwater, in the trees, in the seas, underground, on the seabed, at night, black and white, spots and stripes, large and small, and close to us all. The kids love seeing some of the odd combinations of animals that have been grouped together but, more importantly, it acts as a superb introduction to grouping things together. Consider the questions you could use:

• Are there any other animals that you would add to this group?

• Could you group all of the animals on this page using a different title characteristic?

• Can you split the animals on this page into smaller sub-groups?

---

17 They both have horns.
18 They both live in trees.
19 Joelle Jolivet, *Zoo-ology* (New York: Roaring Brook Press, 2003).

- Can you split any of your sub-groups into further sub-groups?

This leads nicely into methods for presenting and interpreting groups or sets. The Venn diagram is usually comprised of two or more circles, each of which represent a different characteristic. Items that display these characteristics are placed in the appropriate circle. What makes Venn diagrams interesting is that the circles overlap, meaning that you can show both similarities and differences. Anything that does not possess any of the characteristics of any of the groups is placed outside the circles.

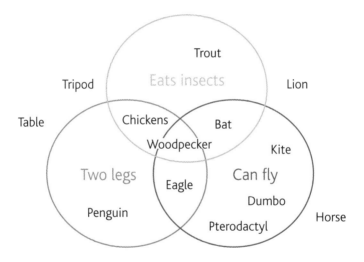

A Carroll diagram is another way to sort things and often takes the form of a grid. This grid is used to sort things in against yes/no criteria (e.g. can breathe underwater/cannot breathe underwater or eats fish/doesn't eat fish). Although Carroll diagrams can contain just one yes/no category, they often contain two categories:

	Breathes underwater	Does not breath underwater
Eats fish	Shark	Alligator
Does not eat fish	Basking Shark	Lion

When asking pupils to sort things, I find it is more effective if they are provided with the items to sort, but have to make up the categories themselves. The children are far more engaged when they get to decide on their own criteria and it is more interesting having items grouped in a variety of ways. This can be easily achieved by providing pupils with blank Venn or Carroll diagram templates. Even better, though, is creating giant versions of the diagrams with hula-hoops for the Venn diagrams and the Carroll diagrams being constructed by using skipping ropes, metre rulers, sports cones, masking tape or playground chalk.[20] In terms of what to get them to sort, I try wherever possible to get actual physical objects: a variety of fruit and vegetables works well, as do toys, stationery, books and even the children themselves.

---

20   Just ask your friendly head of PE first before stealing their stash.

SO, WHAT'S THE CHANCE OF THAT HAPPENING THEN?

Lottery: A tax on people who are bad at math.

Ambrose Bierce

Probability is the likelihood of something happening. The probability of an event happening is calculated by dividing the number of ways it could happen by the total number of possible outcomes. This means that the chance of rolling a normal six-sided dice once and getting the number 3 is one in six because there is only one way you can roll a 3 out of six possible outcomes. At the time of writing, probability is off the national curriculum menu for primary aged pupils. So, why am I bothering to write about it? Well, because it's a superb area of mathematics and one that, in my experience, primary pupils absolutely love. So, bear with me for this short but sweet section on probability, which I promise won't mention anything about flipping a coin. Go on, you know it's worth the risk!

The best way to get children learning about probability is to take a school trip to the local bookies. Only joking! That is a ridiculous idea. But there is often something that can be gleaned from even the most ridiculous of ideas. Surely, part of our moral obligation as teachers is to try, wherever possible, to help our children to make informed decisions about all manner of things, and appropriate risk-taking should be one of those things. The terms 'gambling' and 'risk-taking' can be used interchangeably, but the former is generally frowned on within the school environment. But why not take a look at gambling? I'm not suggesting that the children start wagering their loom bands on who will get full marks in their times tables, nor am I suggesting that you teach your pupils the odds of being dealt a royal flush in five-card poker,[21] but spending a little time looking at how all gambling is set up to make you lose sounds like a good idea to me.

When I was a kid, we used to go to the arcades on the pier in Felixstowe after we had been to the dentist. Like most seaside arcades, this was a properly desperate place, but as a kid the neon glow that emanated from the door, even in daylight, was mesmerising and quickly made you forget all about the fact you had just been told that you were going to need another filling. My mum would give me a pound to spend and I would usually spend five or so minutes doing a circuit around the arcade considering my options: car racing, shoot 'em up, air hockey? The thing is, I always had a look around but I already knew where my money was going. Strolling to the change counter my pound coin was exchanged for a plastic bag of 50 2p pieces. The next 15 minutes would be spent feeding the contents of this bag into the 2p coin pusher machines. I always looked for the machine that had the most coins teetering on the edge, convincing myself that today was going to be my big pay-out. I would watch eagerly as the shelf rocked backwards and forwards, nudging the coins ever closer to the edge. The delight of hearing the clatter of coins hitting the tray beneath was unbeatable. However, this joy was always short lived because no matter which machine I picked, I never left the arcade with anything more than an empty plastic bag. In the grand scheme of things, 'the house' always wins.

One of the best ways to illustrate the basic idea of probability to your pupils requires nothing more than a waste paper bin, some scrap paper and a ball of string. Start the lesson by giving all of the pupils a sheet of A4 scrap paper and asking them to scrunch it up into a ball. Tell the pupils that they will each have one attempt at throwing their paper ball into the bin and that they have to throw from where they are currently sitting, one after the other. Ask the pupils to predict who will be able to get their paper ball in the

---

21 649740:1.

bin. The kids will almost certainly pick their mate who is awesome at football.[22] Once one person gets a few votes the majority of the class will follow but, nevertheless, you still have to ask the children to justify their choice. Next, place the bin as far away as possible from the person that the majority of the children have picked. Some children will have an unfair advantage; they will be closer to the bin. Ask whether they still agree with their first prediction and why. Then it is time to ready, aim, fire!

Following the first volley of paper projectiles, I ask the pupils to think of as many ways as possible that I could increase the likelihood of them getting their paper in the bin. Moving the bin closer? Making the bin bigger? Having more than one shot? All of these suggestions will improve the odds of them getting it in. I also ask the children if they can think of any ways that I could make it less likely for them to get their paper in the bin. I have had suggestions such as making them close their eyes, taking the shot facing backwards by throwing it over their head and moving the bin as the shot is taken. We draw a probability line on the board, which is like a number line, but also illustrates the likelihood of something happening. We plot our suggestions for increasing and decreasing likelihood on the line:

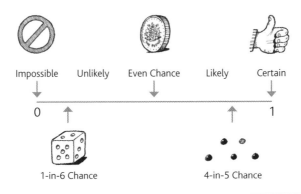

---

22 Is being able to effect a dive into the penalty area a transferable skill that will help here?

However, the important point is that increasing or decreasing the likelihood does not guarantee either success or failure. There is always a risk involved.

So, taking risks is to be avoided, right? Well, not really because we take risks every day, from crossing the road to eating school dinners. It is about selecting which risks are worth taking and then doing everything possible to manage that risk. I have a few simple games I like to play to reinforce this. The first is called Would You Risk It?, where I give a pupil a potentially risky scenario such as, "You've found a packet of your favourite sweets left open on the pavement. Would you risk it?", and they have to reply with whether they would risk it or not. The rest of the class then have a discussion to decide just how risky this is and whether they have made a good decision or not. A slight variation on this game which incorporates a probability line is, Is It Likely?, where pupils have to rank how likely events are on a probability line or, even better, a probability washing line stretched out along the front of the classroom.

Dice are a fantastic resource for demonstrating simple probability and getting pupils used to expressing probability in numerical terms. A simple experiment that can be done is splitting the class into groups of six and assigning each person in that group a number between 1 and 6. They take it in turns to roll a dice, rolling it 60 times in total, and record the results using a tally chart. Using the tally chart, they then turn their results into a numerical format with the number of successful rolls that they had out of 60 (e.g. 7 out of 60). Theoretically, each number should come up ten times as there is a one in six chance of a specific number coming up and 60 ÷ 6 = 10. However, in reality, this is almost never the case, and it's worthwhile pointing this out to the children. Just because theoretically it should happen, doesn't mean it actually will.

After children have worked in a small group for a while, we have a bit of a class gamble. I show the kids a dice with 20 faces and tell them that they are going to be gambling with me. The stake we are to play for is homework. If they win, they won't get any that day; if they lose they'll get an extra question. I tell them that the game is just the same as the last one, but with a dice that has more faces. They want to roll single digit numbers, whereas I want to roll two digit numbers. We roll the dice 20 times and record the results. I've been lucky: on all but one occasion I have won! Regardless of the result, however, there's always a lesson to be learned. I ask the pupils if it was a fair game. Most will reply that it was, as they had half the numbers and I had half the numbers. Except they didn't have half the numbers. They actually only had the numbers 1 to 9, meaning they had a 9 out of 20 chance of winning. I had the numbers 10 to 20, meaning I had an 11 out of 20 chance. The children feel a little cheated, but in a sort of "I can't believe I fell for that sneaky trick" kind of way. Do I feel bad? Not really, I've taught them a valuable lesson. And, anyway, what harm is three extra homework questions going to do ...

AND FINALLY ...

Thank you for getting to the end of this book. If you take just one idea from it and integrate it into your teaching of primary mathematics then I will be happy. Obviously, I hope that having reached the end of this book you will want to take away a lot more than just one idea to reanimate your practice. What I would really love is for anyone who has read this book to go away and tweak, alter and improve my ideas so that they become personal to you and treasured by the children fortunate enough to benefit from your creativity. I hope that you are now hell-bent on ensuring that primary maths becomes the jewel in your curriculum crown. Finally, I hope that every pupil who goes through your classroom finds their own way of loving mathematics, regardless of their ability, because it truly is the most brilliant of subjects – you just have to let it *shine*.

Appendix

MULTIPLICATION GRIDS

Multiply	2	3	4	5	6	7	8	9	10	11	12
2											
3											
4											
5											
6											
7											
8											
9											
10											
11											
12											

Multiply	6	7	12	2	11	5	8	3	9	4	10
2											
3											
4											
5											
6											
7											
8											
9											
10											
11											
12											

Multiply	6	7	12	2	11	5	8	3	9	4	10
4											
9											
3											
10											
5											
11											
2											
12											
6											
8											
7											

PICTURE BOOKS FOR PRIMARY MATHS

Anno, Mitsumasa (1977). *Anno's Journey* (New York: Philomel).

Anno, Mitsumasa (1999). *All in a Day* (New York: Puffin Books).

Anno, Mitsumasa (1999). *Anno's Magic Seeds* (New York: Puffin Books).

Anno, Mitsumasa (1999). *Anno's Mysterious Multiplying Jar* (New York: Puffin Books).

Beaty, Andrea (2007). *Iggy Peck: Architect* (New York: Harry N. Abrams, Inc.).

Beaty, Andrea (2013). *Rosie Revere Engineer* (New York: Abrams Books for Young Readers).

Briggs, Raymond (1997). *Jim and the Beanstalk* (New York: Puffin Books).

Broom, Jenny (2013). *Walk This World* (Somerville, MA: Big Picture Press).

Elliot, David (2013). *Henry's Map* (New York: Philomel/Penguin).

Fromental, Jean-Luc (2007). *365 Penguins* (New York: Harry N. Abrams, Inc.).

Gravett, Emily (2010). *The Rabbit Problem* (London: Macmillan Children's Books).

Hopgood, Tim (2013). *Big!* (London: Picture Corgi).

Jeffers, Oliver (2009). *The Great Paper Caper* (London: HarperCollins Children's Books).

Jeffers, Oliver (2011). *Stuck* (London: HarperCollins Children's Books).

Jenkins, Steve (2011). *Actual Size* (New York: Harcourt Brace and Co.).

Jenkins, Steve (2011). *Just a Second* (New York: Houghton Mifflin Harcourt).

Jolivet, Joelle (2003). *Zoo-ology* (New York: Roaring Brook Press).

Minhos Martins, Isabel and Madalena Matoso (2012). *At Our House* (London: Tate Publishing).

Mizielinska, Aleksandra and Mizielinski, Daniel (2013). *Maps* (Somerville, MA: Big Picture Press).

Perrin, Clotilde (2014). *At the Same Moment Around the World* (San Francisco, CA: Chronicle).

Pinczes, Eleanor. J. (1995). *A Remainder of One* (Boston: Houghton Mifflin Company).

Preston-Gannon, Frann (2012). *The Journey Home* (London: Anova/Pavilion Children's Books).

Rogers, Simon (2014). *Information Graphics: Human Body* (Dorking: Big Picture Press).

Rogers, Simon (2014). *Information Graphics: Animal Kingdom* (Dorking: Big Picture Press).

Smith, David J. (2012). *If the World Were a Village: A Book about the World's People* (Toronto: Kids Can Press).

Tompert, Ann (1998). *Grandfather Tang's Story: A Tale Told with Tangrams* (New York: Crown Publications/Dragonfly Books).

INDEX

Praise for *How to Teach: Primary Maths*

A myriad of creative approaches to mathematics which can be implemented directly or give inspiration to develop our own ideas (in maths and, indeed, across all subject areas). I devoured this book and all the lively ideas within, like the steak-eating crocodile Nick describes. Even better, this is an authentic account of how Nick teaches and if you have never seen a teacher dressed up as a Division Bus, now is the time...

Kate Ryan, GEMS Americas

As someone whose own experiences of primary school maths could certainly be described as 'beige', I found this book to be both refreshing and invigorating. Nick interweaves his passion for primary maths teaching, his belief in its relevance to our 'real' lives and hands-on practical activities in this energising tome that would no doubt make even the most battle-weary of maths teachers want to chuck out their worksheet and re-plan for Monday morning. Nick draws upon various current educational priorities in creating this recipe for primary maths teaching, including the importance of creativity in education (from which maths is not exempt!), the need to develop resilient learners, the essential nature of problem-solving in maths education and the fundamental importance of developing a sound number sense at an early age.

Lucy Moonen, Assistant Head Teacher, Radnor House School

What a wonderful book this is; so much common sense and many imaginative ways to capture the interest of children for the more dreary mathematical topics. It has the perfect balance of rigour and story to provide a more enriching mathematical experience for young learners.

I used to wonder how Nick teaches such outstanding lessons and finally I have a book detailing all his secrets.

Yuvraj Nirwal, Head of Mathematics Key Stage 2–5, Radnor House School